# 1 MONTH OF FREE READING

at

www.ForgottenBooks.com

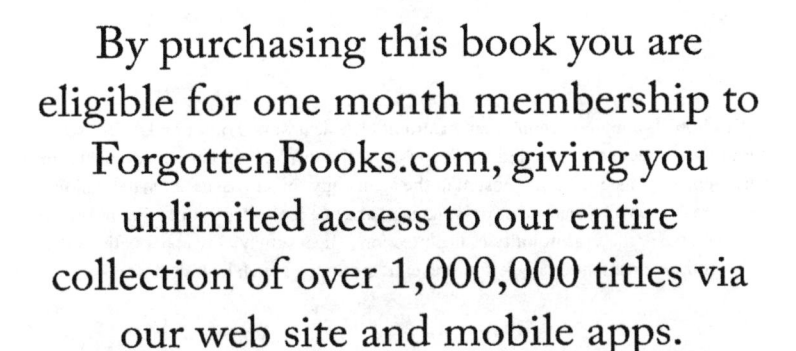

By purchasing this book you are eligible for one month membership to ForgottenBooks.com, giving you unlimited access to our entire collection of over 1,000,000 titles via our web site and mobile apps.

To claim your free month visit:
www.forgottenbooks.com/free910699

\* Offer is valid for 45 days from date of purchase. Terms and conditions apply.

ISBN 978-0-266-92508-8
PIBN 10910699

This book is a reproduction of an important historical work. Forgotten Books uses state-of-the-art technology to digitally reconstruct the work, preserving the original format whilst repairing imperfections present in the aged copy. In rare cases, an imperfection in the original, such as a blemish or missing page, may be replicated in our edition. We do, however, repair the vast majority of imperfections successfully; any imperfections that remain are intentionally left to preserve the state of such historical works.

Forgotten Books is a registered trademark of FB &c Ltd.
Copyright © 2018 FB &c Ltd.
FB &c Ltd, Dalton House, 60 Windsor Avenue, London, SW19 2RR.
Company number 08720141. Registered in England and Wales.

For support please visit www.forgottenbooks.com

# Introductory

IN PRESENTING this catalogue to our customers, we very briefly describe and illustrate a few varieties of nursery stock that our limited space admits.

We are located at the corner of East Church Road and Township Line, one and three-fourths miles east of Elkins Park; three-fourths of a mile west of Ryers Station, P. N. & N. Y. Branch of the Reading Railroad; one mile west of the Fox Chase trolley, at Cottman Street.

Our collection, at present, numbers about one thousand varieties that are considered hardy in this section. We are constantly in communication with home and foreign nurserymen, enabling us, each season, to secure new and rare as well as staple varieties of stock, and shall continue to increase this collection by the addition of varieties of merit, such as we would feel justified in offering to our patrons.

Our stock receives constant, personal attention, being frequently transplanted to insure an excellent root-system, and such as require it are sheared to produce dense, compact specimens.

We can supply a large number of specimen Evergreen, Deciduous and Fruit Trees and Shrubs.

It is our intention to sell the best stock at the lowest prices consistent with the quality of goods offered, all of which we guarantee to be in a healthy condition at the time of delivery. There our obligation ceases, as the future of a tree or plant depends largely on the future care and treatment. If a tree or plant is insured by the grower, a large percentage of the buyers will give no attention whatever to the stock. This applies especially to frequent watering during periods of drought.

*Pine burlaped for shipping*

**WE EMPLOY NO AGENTS OR SALESMEN**

When stock arrives, it should be heeled-in in the ground and plenty of water thrown on the roots. After planting, water is one of the first and most important factors in the success of a plant and must be used freely, especially when the ground is dry. A little water on the surface is of no avail, the ground must be kept moist until the plant is thoroughly established, which means, nearly all of the first summer.

No tree of any kind will thrive if allowed to swing about; this is a point very often overlooked.

Deciduous trees and shrubs, fruit trees and, especially, grape-vines are much improved by pruning, at the time of planting.

We can furnish plans and estimates for plantings, large or small. We can refer prospective buyers to some of the largest and most successful plantings in this vicinity and elsewhere, which were planned and planted by us. We have also furnished trees and shrubs for many of the largest estates.

We request buyers to visit our Nursery, if possible, and make their own selections.

Our Nursery is closed on Sundays.

Freight and Express office, Cheltenham, Pa., P. N. & N. Y. R. R.

While we exercise every care to have our stock true to name, we give no guaranty, and it is mutually agreed between the purchaser and ourselves that we shall, at no time, be held liable for a greater amount than the original price paid for the tree or plant.

Address all correspondence to

## JAMES KREWSON & SONS
### Cheltenham, Montgomery Co., Pa.

*Spruce burlaped for shipping*

# Evergreen Trees

Our stock of evergreen trees consists of many varieties not enumerated in this catalogue, and we are constantly adding more. Our evergreens are sheared about the last of May or during June of each year; this makes them strong and compact. We transplant them to increase their fibrous root-systems, which helps to retain the ball of earth that we burlap when the trees are dug for delivery. We have more than fifty thousand evergreens in stock, and can refer to numerous successful and beautiful plantings taken from our nursery. Evergreens always add very much to the appearance of any place, large or small. The demand for them is constantly and rapidly increasing.

After planting, evergreens need much water, until they are established in the soil. We find that after-care has much to do with the success of them. Large plants must be staked firmly, as swinging about will cause failure. When planted in groups, they must be sheared once a year; this keeps them compact and does much to prevent crowding.

The Retinosporas, Dwarf Arborvitæs and small-growing Junipers are especially good for making beds or grouping. We have, at all times, small evergreens for window- or porch-boxes, and hundreds of large specimens, in many varieties, ready for immediate effect. Some of these are the product of many years' care and transplanting.

## Abies · Fir

**Balsamea** (Balsam Fir; Balm of Gilead). Green foliage; underparts silver.

**Cephalonica.** A large-growing Silver Fir, having the needles arranged in circles around the branches. The needles are short, roundish and sharp.

Abies concolor (see page 2)

## EVERGREEN TREES — JAMES KREWSON & SONS

*Cedrus Deodar aaurea*

#### ABIES, continued

**Concolor.** Very distinct; has a decided grayish blue color; needles are long, clean and healthy looking. The tree always presents a neat appearance, as it never retains dead needles.

**Fraseri** (Fraser's Silver Fir). Similar to the Balsam Fir, except that it has longer needles.

**Nobilis glauca.** A very blue-colored, slow-growing Fir.

**Nordmanniana** (Nordmann's Silver Fir). Has long, glossy, dark green, flat needles, gray underneath. The needles are set at opposites, forming a flat branch. The tree is a very handsome, noble and symmetrical grower, remaining rich-colored throughout the entire winter.

**Pectinata.** Needles short and stiff; arranged all around the branches; hardy.

**Veitchii.** Green needles, gray underneath; very pretty.

**BIOTA. See Thuya.**

### Cedrus · Cedar

**Atlantica glauca** (Mt. Atlas Cedar). A very beautiful tree of somewhat open habit. The tufts of pretty blue needles are always fresh and bright, never losing color, even in winter; hardy.

**Deodara aurea** (Golden Indian Cedar). A rapid grower; rather long needles of a yellowish cast; branches droop somewhat.

#### CEDRUS, continued

**Libani** (Cedar of Lebanon). A very pretty, rich green tree, of rather open habit. Is apt to freeze back somewhat when young, but when once started it seems to thrive excellently.

### Cupressus · Cypress

**Lawsoniana.** A beautiful green; feathery branched and compact.

**Lawsoniana alumii.** A blue form of the above variety; open, feathery habit of growth.

**Triumph of Boskoop.** Bluish color; sturdy and beautiful. One of the best.

### Juniperus · Juniper

**Canadensis.** A spreading, low-growing variety; silvery green, assuming bronze shadings in winter.

**Canadensis aurea** (Douglas' Golden Juniper). Very remarkable and distinct variety, of low habit, breaking forth in the spring a rich golden hue surmounting a silvery green foliage below. In the winter it becomes the most beautiful shades of bronze. Excellent for planting anywhere in the open sunlight, on either high or low ground.

**Chinensis** (Chinese Juniper). Dark green foliage; pyramidal habit; good and hardy.

*Juniperus Virginiana*

Picea excelsa

**JUNIPERUS**, continued

**Chinensis argentea.** Blue-green with little yellow tips dotted among the foliage; pyramidal habit; very choice; hardy.

**Chinensis communis variegata.** A pretty tree, with its sprays of white dotted among the green; rapid grower, becoming pyramidal.

**Elegantissima aurea** (Lee's Golden Juniper). Upright habit and of rapid growth; hardy.

**Erecta.** Very tall; quick grower; bright. Particularly fine for formal effect.

**Hibernica** (Irish Juniper). Grayish green; good, compact grower of pyramidal habit.

**Japonica aurea.** Of irregular, spreading habit, low growth and of the richest yellow the entire year. Grows in almost any situation.

**Pfitzeriana.** A newer variety of much merit. Is of the Savin habit, but of a darker, richer color and more robust growth. This Juniper is much admired.

**Sabina** (Savin Juniper). Rich green, dagger-like branches. Fine for rockeries, banks or any place where an irregular plant is wanted.

**Sabina variegata** (Variegated Savin Juniper). Green, with yellowish white spots dotted among the branches; of irregular, low growth.

**Schotti.** Rich, cheerful green; of erect habit and is hardy.

**Suecica** (Swedish Juniper). Blue-gray in color; fairly rapid, erect growth.

**Suecica nana** (Dwarf Swedish Juniper). Bluish green; compact branches, slightly curled on ends; very pretty and interesting.

**JUNIPERUS**, continued

**Virginiana** (Red Cedar). This tree has many uses and is being more generally planted. It is a tall, erect grower and very hardy, even near the sea.

**Virginiana glauca.** A very pleasing tree, of rich blue color all the year. Is very hardy and will thrive anywhere an evergreen could be expected to grow. It is very popular in groups of evergreens, where a blue plant is wanted. We sell large numbers of this variety each season.

## Picea · Spruce

**Alba** (White Spruce). A very compact-growing variety; green to grayish green; short needles. One of the best-known evergreens.

**Alcockiana** (Alcock's Spruce). A curious tree of medium size, with short green needles, blue-gray underneath.

**Douglasii** (Douglas' Spruce). One of the rapid growers, and is a very pretty tree, with a somewhat feathery aspect.

**Engelmanni** (Engelmann's Spruce). Of very pretty, compact habit; hardy.

**Excelsa** (Norway Spruce). A fast grower; very good where quick effect is demanded; can be improved by shearing. We offer thousands of these, in sizes from little trees to large ones, 10 to 12 feet high.

**Excelsa aurea** (Golden Norway Spruce). Branches slightly tinged with gold.

Picea pungens glauca (see page 4)

## Pinus · Pine

**Austriaca** (Austrian Pine). A valuable and much-admired tree. The long, straight needles are of a rich green and borne two in a sheath; is very hardy and of quick growth. Needles are about 4 to 5 inches long.

**Banksiana** (Jack Pine). A very compact, rather slow-growing tree, with two needles, about 1 inch long, in a sheath; grayish green color; very hardy and pleasing.

**Cembra** (Swiss Stone Pine). A very slow, compact grower; robust and always pleasing; five needles, 3 to 4 inches long, in a sheath; resembles a miniature White Pine.

**Corsica.** A very interesting, tall-growing Pine; has long, crimpy needles, about 5 inches long, borne in two a sheath and are dark green; very hardy and free from diseases.

**Excelsa** (Bhotan Pine). Five drooping gray needles, 6 to 8 inches long, are found in each sheath; the tree grows quite rapidly and is very beautiful, always having a graceful appearance; it is very hardy and never loses its color, even in the coldest weather.

**Mugho** (Dwarf Mountain Pine). A very popular, low-growing plant, of a pretty green color. There are two needles, about 2 inches long, in a sheath. This is a particularly valuable Pine for planting at the house foundation or at the corners of paths and drives, where it soon forms a broad, low, evergreen bush, with the twigs standing upright.

Pinus Mugho

### PICEA, continued

**Excelsa inversa** (Weeping Norway Spruce). A very striking tree. Branches decidedly weeping and assuming grotesque shapes. A quaint lawn tree. We offer some good specimens.

**Excelsa pendula** (Drooping Norway Spruce). Main branches growing horizontal and the lateral branches being pendulous, giving the tree a graceful appearance.

**Excelsa pygmæa.** A very dwarf, green Spruce, fine for grouping at corners.

**Excelsa Remonti.** A dwarf, compact variety for planting in front of the tall-growing evergreens.

**Nigra** (Black Hills Spruce). A rich green species, somewhat like *Picea excelsa*, but darker.

**Orientalis** (Oriental Spruce). Of slower growth than *Picea excelsa*; has a rich, glossy, dark green color all the year. A very good variety and cannot be too highly recommended for exposed places, as it is extremely hardy, resisting any extreme of weather after it is established.

**Polita** (Tiger's Tail Spruce). A very stiff, hardy tree, with long piercing needles of a rich green. Slow grower.

**Pungens** (Colorado Spruce). A very hardy tree of green color; compact habit of growth; needles sharp and penetrating.

**Pungens glauca** (Colorado Blue Spruce). Varies in color from a greenish gray to the richest blue; very hardy and of compact growth. A handsome tree.

**Pungens glauca Kosteri** (Koster's Blue Spruce). This is the richest blue of them all, and retains its color throughout the year. We offer a large stock of these pretty trees, in many sizes, at very attractive prices.

**Pungens Parryana glauca.** A blue strain of the *Picea pungens*; of fine color and symmetrical habit; hardy and very desirable.

Pinus Strobus

*PINUS, continued*

**Ponderosa** (Bull Pine). Needles 8 to 9 inches long; a very striking tree; hardy and distinct.

**Strobus** (Common White Pine). Of great value particularly on large places; rapid grower; needles, which always grow five in a sheath, are 3 to 4 inches long, and are of a gray-green color.

**Sylvestris** (Scotch Pine). Very hardy, practically immune from diseases or extremes of weather; a very pretty tree with needles 2 inches long, borne two in a sheath, and of a grayish green color.

**Tanyosho** (Japanese Table Pine). A curious little bushy Pine, growing low and dense; perfectly flat on top, hence the name.

## Podocarpus

**Koraiana** (Japan Yew). Very pretty dark green, with long needles and of pyramidal habit.

## Retinospora · Japan Cypress

A valuable group of evergreens, with many variations of type and color; used for specimens, for grouping or in beds; they are hardy and stand shearing, which adds much to their value, making them compact and beautiful. We offer many varieties, some of which are described as follows:

**Filicoides.** Of slender growth; has short, rather fern-like foliage, of a rich green.

**Filifera.** Foliage thread-like, drooping and graceful; dark, lustrous green and retaining a good rich green the entire winter; of fairly rapid growth.

Retinospora squarrosa Veitchii (see page 6)

*RETINOSPORA, con.*

**Filifera aurea.** A golden form of Filifera, but inclined to get breadth rather than height; it is of the most pronounced golden color the entire year.

**Filiformis.** A newer sort of Japan Cypress; has long, plume-like, drooping branches of light green; very graceful and distinct.

**Obtusa.** A fine tree, with glossy foliage of a dark green shade; maintains its color even in the coldest weather.

**Obtusa aurea.** A golden yellow form of *R. obtusa.*

**Obtusa gracilis.** A pretty, graceful little tree of richest coloring; the branches have a slightly drooping habit; a valuable and useful plant for entrance plantings.

Retinospora burlaped for shipping

**Obtusa gracilis aurea.** A lighter-colored form than the above, but having the same habit, and grows about the same height.

**Obtusa lycopodioides.** A very dwarf variety; rich green, taking the lightest tinge of purple in winter; rare.

**Obtusa nana.** A very dwarf variety, of compact growth, with chunky, obtuse branches; really miniature trees; color rich green.

**Obtusa nana aurea.** Very dwarf; a golden form of Obtusa nana.

**Pisifera.** Of rapid growth; rich green and handsome; branches droop somewhat at ends; hardy.

**Pisifera aurea.** One of the most distinct of the larger-growing, golden foliaged Retinosporas; its color is very pronounced, having rich, golden tipped, graceful branches, which maintain their color the entire year, always imparting a refreshing relief to the heavier colors, especially in winter; also giving grace to the stiffer varieties when they are grouped together; very hardy and is much improved by shearing.

## Taxus · Yew

**Baccata** (English Yew). Dark green; broad habit of growth.
**Baccata aurea** (Golden English Yew). Rich yellow in color and much admired.
**Cuspidata brevifolia.** Rich green; needles rather short; hardy.
**Procumbens.** A low, spreading shrub; foliage rich green; very attractive. Good for the front of the evergreen planting.
**Repandens.** A creeping form, with rich green foliage; very hardy.

## Thuya · Arborvitae

**Occidentalis** (American Arborvitæ). Of rapid growth; does not transplant as easily as *T. pyramidalis*; low in cost.
**Occidentalis, Columbia.** A very pretty variety, with white tips, becoming more pronounced as season advances.
**Occidentalis compacta.** Dense; of a pretty light green; excellent for small groups, window-boxes, hedges, etc.
**Occidentalis ericoides** (Heath Arborvitæ). Very dwarf and compact; feathery foliage, which is green in summer, changing to purplish brown in winter.

*Retinospora plumosa*

### RETINOSPORA, continued

**Plumosa.** Foliage green and is formed in feathery plumes; excellent; fairly rapid in growth; is much improved by annual shearing.
**Plumosa albo-spica,** or **argentea.** A very distinct member of this useful family and is the subject of much admiration; the feathery branches, having white tips, appear as though a light snow had fallen on them.
**Plumosa aurea.** A golden form of *R. plumosa*, growing rather rapidly; very popular for specimens or groups; hardy and easy of culture.
**Plumosa lutescens.** Of dwarf, compact and shapely habit; has light yellow tips and is hardy; an excellent plant for small groups, as it grows very slowly.
**Plumosa sulphurea.** A form of Retinospora much resembling Plumosa aurea, but has much lighter-colored tips and is of much slower growth; compact and hardy.
**Squarrosa Veitchii.** Steel-blue in color during the summer, with a bronze tinge during the winter; a very pretty and distinct Retinospora of close, compact growth.

## Sciadopitys verticillata
### Umbrella Pine

A very hardy and altogether distinct conifer of great beauty; a bunch of long, bright green needles are borne at the end of each branch. A native of Japan.

*Thuya orientalis*

*THUYA, continued*

**Occidentalis gigantea.** Rich, glossy green foliage; upright habit, tall; rapid grower.

**Occidentalis globosa** (Globe Arborvitæ). Real globe-shaped; no trimming needed; dark green and very hardy; a favorite for window-boxes, bordering beds of larger plants, etc.

**Occidentalis Hoveyi.** A dwarfish variety; flat, feathery branches of a light green, becoming lighter at tips; shapely and compact.

**Occidentalis lutea** (George Peabody Arborvitæ). A tall and rather rapid grower, of extreme hardiness; it is bright yellow and maintains its color all the year.

**Occidentalis pyramidalis.** Tall, narrow and lofty of habit; of nice green color; one of the best of the tall Thuyas.

**Occidentalis Reidi.** Similar to *T. Wareana*, excepting that it grows globular instead of pyramidal; compact and of a rich green; very hardy.

**Occidentalis, Tom Thumb.** Compact, dwarf and hardy; foliage feathery and shows two characters on the same plant, the lower part like an Arborvitæ and the top like a Cedar.

Siberian Arborvitæ

*THUYA, continued*

**Occidentalis, Rosedale.** A dainty little dwarf, of excellent shape; pretty green in summer and a purplish color in winter.

**Occidentalis Wareana** (Siberian Arborvitæ). Very hardy; of excellent habit, being compact and of a beautiful, dark green.

**Orientalis** (Chinese Arborvitæ, or *Biota orientalis*). Rich green; pyramidal shape; rapid grower.

**Orientalis compacta.** Pretty green foliage; very dwarf.

**Orientalis elegantissima.** A beautiful golden color in summer, changing to rich shades of bronze, gold and purplish green in winter; very hardy and easy of culture. Like most all highly colored evergreens, it does much better in the open light.

**Orientalis nana aurea** (Berckman's Golden Arborvitæ). Very dwarf and of the richest color; compact and hardy. It is a bright golden until cold weather comes, when it changes to somewhat bronze hues.

## Tsuga

**Canadensis** (Hemlock Spruce). Makes good evergreen hedge and screen, or can be trimmed into elegant specimens. This plant is much in demand. We offer a nice lot in various sizes.

## Wellingtonia

**Gigantea** (The Giant Tree of California). Grows to an immense size. We have been growing a few of these for several years, and notice that they, like the Cedar of Lebanon, are hardy after they get a good start, but should be given a slight protection for the first few years.

Tsuga Canadensis

Kalmia latifolia (see page 9)

## Evergreen Shrubs

Evergreen shrubs are very valuable, as the foliage is to be taken into consideration, as well as the flowers. A large number of the varieties can be planted in exposures where other things would fail. Wonderful results can be obtained by planting them in their proper places. We sell thousands of Rhododendrons, Kalmias, Boxwoods, etc., each year.

### Aucuba

**Japonica.** Large, green leaves, with numerous light spots, making a very beautiful effect. The berries are quite large and of a very bright red. This plant is not hardy in this locality; must be well protected in winter, or taken up with a ball of earth and placed in a cellar or other place where extreme cold does not reach. They can be used to good advantage in winter as an indoor plant, in a cool place, such as a vestibule.

### Andromeda

**Floribunda.** A dwarf evergreen shrub, with bright green leaves; white flowers, in sprays like lily-of-the-valley. One of the most beautiful shrubs for the front of the rhododendron bed. Grows about 2 feet high, and beautiful all year round.

**Japonica.** Buds and foliage are of darker hue than *A. floribunda*, and appear to resist extremes of heat and cold better.

### Azalea

**Amoena.** A very desirable evergreen shrub, with roundish dark green, glossy leaves, which somewhat resemble boxwood in summer, but as the cold weather sets in they assume beautiful shades of bronze. The rich magenta flowers cover the entire plant in May, making it a mass of bloom, often entirely hiding the leaves. *Azalea amoena* seems to thrive in almost any reasonably good soil or situation; best results are obtained by a mulch or partial covering of leaves during a severe winter.

**Hinodigeri.** Resembles *A. amoena*, but has red flowers and somewhat larger leaves.

**Indica alba.** A very beautiful evergreen Azalea. Its clear white flowers are somewhat the shape of *A. mollis*.

**Mollis** and **Pontica.** See Deciduous Shrubs.

### Berberis • Barberry

**Ilicifolia** (Holly-leaved Barberry). Dark green, prickly leaves; curved and spiny.

## Buxus · Boxwood

We make a specialty of Boxwood, from the small edging plants up to large pyramids; also, standards, globes, obelisks and squares, in various sizes. Boxwoods are the general favorite for vases and for planting where a formal effect is desired. The Boxwoods, with their dark green, glossy leaves are always pleasing; they are long-lived shrubs and many can be seen growing about old places, which have stood for, perhaps, several generations. We shear our Boxwoods during June of each year, which is very necessary to retain shape and beauty and also give strength to the plant. Boxwood, or any evergreen, planted in a vase or tub, dries out quickly and requires frequent watering.

**Sempervirens.** Used in formal gardens either in tubs or planted out, and grows rather slowly.

Bushes from 1 ft. up to 3 ft.
Pyramids from 2 ft. up to 6 ft.
Globes from 1 x 1 ft. up to 2½ x 2½ ft.
Obelisks, squares, standards, various sizes.

**Suffruticosa** (Dwarf Box). The old-fashioned box edging. We offer this in nice plants with good roots.

Buxus sempervirens (Pyramidal Box)

Daphne Cneorum (Garland Flower)

## Daphne

**Cneorum** (Garland Flower). This little shrub is too little known and should have much more attention. Planted in a sheltered position, it rewards us, in the early spring, with the most deliciously fragrant, pink blossoms.

## Ilex · Holly

We make a specialty of Hollies, and offer each spring a nice lot at very low prices.

**Crenata** (Japanese Holly). Has small leaves; very hardy.

**Aquifolium** (English Holly). Beautiful, dark, glossy green leaves, gracefully curved and spiny; rapid grower.

**Aquifolium pyramidalis.** Very pretty green leaves and said to be more certain to bear berries.

**Aquifolium variegata.** Beautiful variegated leaves; often found with berries.

## Kalmia · Laurel

**Latifolia** (Common Laurel, or Calico Bush). A native of our woods. Has very pretty pink flowers during May.

## Mahonia

**Aquifolium** (Holly-leaved Mahonia). A very desirable shrub with many uses. As a companion to deciduous shrubs, or with the boxwoods; rhododendrons and azaleas, it gives pleasing results. Again, it is sometimes used for making small hedges. The beautiful holly-like leaves change from rich, glossy green in summer, to the most beautiful bronze and red in winter. In very early spring a spike of yellow bloom sometimes is seen, which is followed by a crop of berries which turn purple.

## Rhododendrons

We make these beautiful evergreen shrubs a specialty, selling each season thousands of them. They like a rather cool, moist, partly shaded situation. When we consider their handsome, broad, glossy, dark green foliage and their beautiful flowers, in such a variety of colors, they cannot be estimated too highly. Rhododendrons should have a mulch of well-rotted manure, or plenty of leaves thrown liberally among them.

**Catawbiense.** This is an excellent sort for general planting; the foliage is rich green, always pleasing and vigorous; it is hardy, grows compact and is a profuse bloomer. The flowers vary somewhat, from lilac to old-rose in color. We always have large quantities of this variety, in sizes from 1 foot up, some of them quite broad and well set with buds.

**Cunninghami.** White; very bushy, compact grower. Must have a rather sheltered situation.

**Maximum.** This is our native mountain Rhododendron, or Giant Laurel. Blooms about midsummer in shades from pale rose to deep pink.

**Punctatum.** Very dwarf; small leaves; pink flowers. Fine for the border of a Rhododendron bed.

### HYBRID RHODODENDRONS

**Alarm.** White, scarlet center.
**Abraham Lincoln.** Soft rose.
**Album elegans.** White.
**Album grandiflorum.** Buds pink, opening white; strong, vigorous and profuse budder, flowers open beautifully; foliage excellent; very hardy and good grower.
**Anna Parsons.** Reddish pink.
**Blandianum.** Red; very hardy.
**Boule de Neige.** Dwarf; pure white; foliage unsurpassed; very hardy.
**Candidissima.** White.
**Caractacus.** Crimson; a great favorite; very hardy; profuse bloomer.
**Charles Dickens.** Bright red; good, hardy variety.
**Delicatissima.** White.
**Everestianum.** Lilac-rose; good budder and blooms open nicely; excellent foliage; one of the very best; hardy.
**Fastuosum.** Double; purple; very large truss, flowers often cover entire foliage; the leaves are thick, oval and rich-colored.
**Giganteum.** Red.
**H. W. Sargent.** Carmine-red.
**James Bateman.** Scarlet.
**John Spencer.** Violet-rose; very striking foliage; hardy.
**Kettledrum.** Red; hardy.
**Lady Armstrong.** Pink; hardy.
**Lady Clermont.** Reddish pink.
**Luciferum.** White.
**Madame Carvalho.** A good white variety.
**Michael Waterer.** Bright red.
**Mrs. Milner.** Bright red; hardy.
**Old Port.** Brownish red; hardy.
**Parson's Grandiflorum.** Red.
**Pres. Lincoln.** Rosy purple; large flower-truss; hardy.
**Roseum elegans.** Pink; hardy.
**Roseum superbum.** Rose.

Avenue of Norway Maples (Acer platanoides)

## Deciduous Trees

### Acer · Maple

**Campestre** (English Cork-bark Maple). Small and slow-growing.

**Colchicum rubrum.** A Japanese tree, with pretty crimson leaves, changing to rich green. A very pretty small tree.

**Crispum.** A variety with crimped leaves.

**Dasycarpum.** (Silver Maple). Fast grower; leaves have a silvery color underneath.

**Dasycarpum pyramidalis** (Pyramidal Silver Maple). Tall, erect grower.

**Ginnala.** Low-growing, bushy tree, or large shrub.

**Lonbergii.** A Norway Maple, with deeply cut leaves.

**Negundo** (Box Elder). Rapid grower in any soil; has leaves resembling the ash.

**Platanoides** (Norway Maple). A beautiful tree, compact and healthy; grows in almost any reasonable situation. It does not thrive in wet or swampy places, however. One of the most popular trees for street planting in the suburbs.

**Platanoides cucullata.** A species of Norway Maple, with curious, curly leaves.

**Platanoides globosa** (Globe Norway Maple). A small, round, formal tree of recent introduction.

**Platanoides Schwedleri** (Schwedler's Norway Maple). A species having red, or purplish red, leaves in early spring and turning to dark green as they expand. We offer an elegant collection.

Acer polymorphum (Japan Maples). See page 12

## DECIDUOUS TREES — JAMES KREWSON & SONS

*ACER, continued*

**Platanoides Reitenbachi.** A variety of Norway Maple with purplish leaves.

**Pseudo-platanus** (European Sycamore Maple). Has dark bark and darker and thicker leaves than the Norway.

**Pseudo-platanus Leopoldi.** Has green and yellowish variegated leaves throughout the summer. On close examination one can scarcely find two leaves exactly alike.

**Saccharinum** (Sugar Maple). A handsome tree; does not grow so dense as the Norway Maple; takes pretty autumn colors; straight, upright grower.

**Rubrum** (Swamp or Red Maple). A beautiful tree in autumn, with its wonderful colorings; the bright red buds give color and cheer in the first days of spring.

### Japan Maples

Like most foliage plants, better-colored leaves are obtained on Japan Maples by planting in the open; a shady place tends to mar the brighter color of the leaves. They are hardy, entirely free from insect pests and very satisfactory, whether in groups, singly as specimens, or planted with other shrubs.

**Aureum.** Beautifully cut, golden leaves; slow grower; dwarf.

**Polymorphum.** Forms a large shrub and gets a beautiful autumn color.

**Polymorphum atropurpureum.** Red-leaf Japan Maple.

**Polymorphum atropurpureum nigrum.** A new red variety.

**Polymorphum dissectum.** Reddish cut-leaf.

**Polymorphum dissectum viridis.** Green cut-leaf.

Catalpa Bungei

Betula alba pendula (Cut-leaf Weeping Birch)

### Æsculus · Buckeye; Horse-Chestnut

**Hippocastanum** (European Horse-Chestnut). A round-headed tree; white flowers in early June.

**Hippocastanum Briotti.** Deep red flowers.

**Hippocastanum flore albo-plena.** Double White-flowering Horse-Chestnut. Blooms in late May or early June.

**Rubicunda.** Red-flowered Horse-Chestnut.

### Aralia

**Spinosa** (Hercules' Club). A robust, tropical looking plant with pinnate leaves 3 feet in length; has plumes of white blossoms in summer, followed by a crop of dark berries.

### Asimina

**Triloba** (Papaw Tree.) A small tree, with handsome foliage, and large flowers in early spring. Bears quaint, spicy fruits.

### Betula · Birch

**Alba** (White Birch). A very pretty lawn tree.

**Alba pendula** (Cut-leaf Weeping Birch). Has white bark; pretty green cut leaves on graceful, drooping branches.

# CHELTENHAM, PENNSYLVANIA — DECIDUOUS TREES

Ginkgo biloba (Maidenhair Tree). See page 14

## Carpinus

**Caroliniana** (Hornbeam; Ironwood). Makes a good screen; has compact, rich green foliage, turning brown in autumn and remaining on all winter; hardy; will succeed almost anywhere.

## Catalpa

**Bungei.** See Weeping and Formal Trees and Shrubs.

**Speciosa.** Has large, handsome leaves that give a tropical aspect to this rapid-growing tree; spikes of purplish tinted white flowers, a foot or more long, appear in June. The long pendent seed-pods give it the popular name of Candle Tree.

## Cedrela

**Sinensis.** A pretty tree of a rather low, spreading habit, with a dense growth; pinnate leaves and large sprays of white flowers.

## Cerasus · Cherry

The flowering Cherry is a valuable, small-growing tree. Its pretty, rich green foliage remains green late in autumn; the handsome double pink or white flowers are borne in great abundance all over the tree.

**Japonica flore-pleno, Pink.** Double pink flowers; blooms in May.

*CERASUS, continued*

**Japonica flore-pleno, White.** Double white flowers; blooms in May.

**James Veitch.** Double pink flowers; blooms in May.

## Cercis

**Canadensis** (American Judas, or Red Bud). A small tree, with pink flowers covering the tree in spring.

**Japonica.** See Shrubs.

## Cercidiphyllum

**Japonicum** (Japanese Kadsura). A pyramidal-growing tree, with pretty, roundish leaves of rich green color.

## Cladrastis

**Tinctoria** (Yellow-wood, or *Virgilia lutea*). Pendulous branches and sprays of compact foliage.

## Cornus · Dogwood

**Florida** (White Dogwood). White flowers in early spring; red berries in autumn.

**Florida rubra** (Pink-flowering Dogwood). A very striking tree when in flower; also bears red fruit. A great favorite.

## Cytisus Laburnum

A small, slender-growing tree, or large shrub; has greenish bark and bears an abundance of yellow flowers in racemes in June.

Flowers of Cornus florida (Dogwood)

# 14 DECIDUOUS TREES — JAMES KREWSON & SONS

Magnolia Soulangeana

### Diospyros · Persimmon
**Virginiana.** The common Persimmon.
**Kaki.** The large Japanese Persimmon.

### Fagus · Beech
**Asplenifolia** (Fern-leaved Beech). A small, slow-growing, ornamental tree.
**Purpurea** (Purple or Copper-leaved Beech). Easy of culture; of rapid growth and as lasting as an oak; neither storms nor the ravages of time, extremes of heat or cold, affect it. It grows to immense size and is very symmetrical.
**Riversi** (Rivers' Purple Beech). Very dark purple leaves; grows large and compact.
**Sylvatica pendula** (Weeping Beech). A very interesting tree of large growth.
**Sylvatica tricolor.** Has curious foliage of several shades; very small tree, of slow growth.

### Fraxinus · Ash
**Americana** (White Ash). A large, rapid-growing tree, of easy culture.

### Ginkgo
**Biloba** (Maidenhair Tree). An interesting pyramidal-growing tree, with curious leaves of a pleasing appearance. Makes a very handsome tree if properly pruned.

### Gleditschia · Honey Locust
A very hardy, medium-sized tree, bearing pretty foliage and racemes of very fragrant flowers.

### Gymnocladus
**Canadensis** (Kentucky Coffee Tree). A large, open-growing tree, with long, compound leaves; of a tropical aspect; the branches are devoid of twigs.

### Koelreuteria
**Paniculata** (Varnish Tree). Yellow blossoms; compound leaves, which are somewhat sticky, hence the name Varnish Tree. A native of China.

### Larix · Larch
Rapid-growing trees, which are the subject of much admiration in spring, when they send out their pretty, rich green, pine-needle foliage. While not evergreens, they are conifers.
**Europæa.** Broad-spreading and of large growth.
**Kaempferi** (Japanese Larch). Of more erect habit.

Platanus orientalis (Oriental Plane).

All our trees are grown so that they develop the healthiest root systems

### Magnolia

**Acuminata** (Cucumber Tree). A symmetrical, rapid grower; has large, handsome leaves.
**Conspicua.** Bears large, white, sweet-scented flowers in early spring.
**Glauca** (Swamp Magnolia). Sweet-scented white flowers in summer; does well in any good soil.
**Kobus.** A very free-blooming white variety; hardy and robust.
**Lennei.** Reddish purple flowers; sometimes blooms in autumn.
**Soulangeana.** Flowers pink, shaded with white; one of the very prolific bloomers.
**Soulangeana nigra.** Very dark red flowers.
**Tripetala.** A tropical-looking tree, having immense broad leaves; yellowish flowers, which are followed by red, cone-like seed-pods.

### Morus · Mulberry

**Alba Tatarica** (Russian Mulberry). Low-growing tree, with curiously lobed leaves.
**Alba pendula** (Tea's Weeping Mulberry). See Weeping Trees and Shrubs.

### Oxydendrum

**Arboreum** (Sorrel Tree). A pretty tree, with leaves that turn the brightest crimson in autumn; flowers resemble those of lily-of-the-valley; will thrive in any soil.

### Persica · Peach

**Flore-pleno** (Double-flowering Peach). Nothing could be prettier than a tree of Flowering Peach in full bloom; the flowers are of the clearest pink, red or white, and are borne over the entire tree, making it an object of much pleasure and admiration. A delightful tree for planting on the lawn.

Quercus palustris (Pin Oak). See page 16

### Platanus · Plane

**Orientalis** (Oriental Plane). Perhaps the most popular tree for planting in city streets; it will resist conditions where others fail. It is of rapid and symmetrical growth; thrives in soils too wet for Norway maples, and seems to resist smoke and dust. We have a large stock of these trees, of various sizes, to offer.

### Populus · Poplar

**Balsamifera** (Balm of Gilead). Has broader leaves and holds them better than the Carolina Poplar.
**Nigra fastigiata** (Lombardy Poplar). A rapid, pyramidal-growing tree, which holds its leaves splendidly until autumn. This tree has a very large sale and seems to be increasing in popularity; the numerous situations which demand a tall, pyramidal tree quickly, or a tall screen, tend to increase the demand for it.

### Prunus · Plum

**Pissardi.** A very pretty, small-growing tree, with reddish leaves and little pink blossoms, followed by bright red fruit.

### Pyrus

**Ioensis plena** (Bechtel's Double-flowering Crab). Double pink flowers with a sweet perfume.
**Parkmani** (Parkman's Crab). Semi-double pink flowers.

Salix Babylonica (Weeping Willow). See p. 16

## Quercus · Oak

**Alba** (White Oak). A noble tree, attaining great age and large dimensions.
**Cerris** (Turkey Oak). A European variety.
**Palustris** (Pin Oak). One of the most popular Oaks; a very worthy tree.
**Pedunculata** (English Oak). A dense, bushy tree, which holds its leaves in winter.
**Pedunculata fastigiata** (Pyramidal Oak). A good tree; grows pyramidal, much like Lombardy poplar, but of slower growth.
**Phellos** (Willow Oak). A rapid and pretty grower; will thrive in moist or low ground.
**Rubra** (Red Oak). A rapid, robust grower; has large leaves.

## Salix · Willow

**Babylonica** (Weeping Willow). A tree of great value, breaking forth in leaf during the first days of spring and remaining a beautiful, fresh green all summer and fall. There are few trees that grow as fast and, where a large, dense screen is wanted quickly, this Willow will be appreciated. Will succeed in almost any soil, and is well known as one of the most graceful trees in existence.
**Caprea.** A small-growing tree, with good foliage; in early spring it bears numerous little catkins, strewn along the branches at regular intervals.
**Vitellina aurea** (Golden Bark Willow). Very pretty yellow wood in winter.
**Laurifolia** (Laurel-leaved Willow). Has handsome, broad, dark green foliage, which is glossy and makes a pretty appearance. This is a very nice tree, of rapid growth, even in the poorest soil.

## Sophora

**Japonica.** A handsome, small tree of excellent qualities; greenish bark, pinnate foliage; pea-shaped, white flowers appear in drooping clusters in September.

## Sorbus

**Americana** (American Mountain Ash). An interesting and pleasing little tree, having beautiful pinnate foliage and bearing white blossoms in spring, which are followed by orange-colored fruits changing to the brightest scarlet.

## Taxodium

**Distichum** (Deciduous Cypress). A very handsome, spiral tree, of rapid growth, straight and regular habit; has dainty, fern-like foliage.

## Tilia · Linden

**Americana** (American Linden). Large, broad leaves; rapid grower.
**Argentea** (Silver Linden). Leaves are silvery white underneath; a very pretty tree, of excellent form and rapid growth.
**Europæa** (European Linden). A very symmetrical-growing tree; is much admired for its beautiful, round head and compact growth.

## Ulmus · Elm

**Americana** (American Elm). An old favorite, of rapid growth; it becomes a tall, majestic tree of great spread, and is very long-lived.
**Campestris** (English Elm). Somewhat smaller grower than the American Elm.
**Wheatleyi** (Wheatley's Elm). Grows very tall and assumes a pyramidal shape.

American Elms (Ulmus Americana)

# Deciduous Shrubs

### Amelanchier

**Canadensis** (Juneberry). White flowers in late April; purplish berries in July.

### Amorpha

**Fruticosa** (False Indigo). Purple spikes of flowers in June; rather open-growing bush.

### Amygdalus · Flowering Almond

Double pink flowers in May. There is also a double white variety, which blooms the same month.

### Azalea

**Mollis.** A choice collection of seedlings having large flowers, of shades of yellow, salmon, etc.
**Mollis Hybrids.** Assorted colors.
**Pontica Daviesi.** White.
**Pontica narcissiflora.** Yellow.
**Pontica pallas.** Crimson.

### Baccharis · Groundsel Bush

Bears white flowers in September.

### Berberis · Barberry

**Purpurea.** Medium height; purple leaves; very small, pinkish white flowers; berries red.
**Thunbergi** (Japanese Barberry). Low and spreading, yet compact habit; has beautiful foliage and bears bright red berries, which remain during the winter; makes a good hedge and is very popular, only needs trimming once a year. Extremes of weather do not injure it after it is once established. As specimens or in groups, with shearing, it is very pleasing; fine for planting on banks, and even in certain

Berberis Thunbergi, continued
places where many other plants fail it becomes, with a little care, very satisfactory.
**Vulgaris.** Upright growth; green leaves and red berries.

### Benzoin · Spice Bush

Yellow flowers appear in very early spring, before the leaves.

### Buddleia

**Veitchi.** Beautiful spikes of fragrant, purple flowers appear in late summer and remain for a long time.

Azalea mollis

18   DECIDUOUS SHRUBS  JAMES KREWSON & SONS

### Callicarpa

**Purpurea** (Beauty Fruit). Very small flowers of a purplish shade in July, and followed by pretty purple berries, borne in great profusion the entire length of the branches, in autumn.

### Calycanthus

**Floridus** (Sweet Shrub). Has large leaves and brown flowers; blooms in May and at intervals during summer.

### Caragana

**Arborescens** (Siberian Pea). Yellow flowers in May; bark is greenish in color and foliage is pinnate.

### Caryopteris

**Mastacanthus** (Blue Spirea). A neat little shrub, growing 3 to 4 feet high in rich soil, bearing rich blue flowers during August and September. The foliage and flowers present a pleasing effect; as the flowers fade they at once fall, giving place to newer ones. The foliage remains good until the flowers are done.

Chionanthus Virginica (**White Fringe**). See page 19

### Cassia

**Marylandica** (Wild Senna). Spikes of yellow flowers, with reddish spots, in July. Will thrive in almost any situation, and blooms when very few shrubs are in flower.

### Ceanothus

**Americanus** (New Jersey Tea). White flowers in June; attains a height of 3 to 4 feet.

### Cephalanthus
#### Button Bush

Little balls of white flowers appear in July. Very easy of culture in any soil.

### Cercis

**Canadensis.** See Deciduous Trees.

**Japonica** (Japan Judas Tree). In the early spring the branches of this shrub are dotted plentifully with rich, purplish pink blossoms, which resemble small sweet peas. The foliage is of the most beautiful waxy green and not injured by heat or drought.

**Hydrangea arborescens grandiflora** (see page 20)

## Chionanthus

**Virginica** (White Fringe). In June long, drooping panicles of finely cut, fringe-like, white flowers appear among the large foliage. The seeds become purple and are quite large.

## Citrus

**Trifoliata** (Hardy Japan Orange). Fragrant, white flowers; beautiful foliage; the bark is green and studded with long, green thorns. The little oranges are pretty but not edible.

## Clethra

**Alnifolia** (Sweet Pepper Bush). White and very fragrant flowers in early summer; of rather dwarf habit, attaining about 4 feet.

## Colutea

**Arborescens** (Bladder Senna). Yellow flowers in July, followed by curious, bladder-shaped seed-pods; will thrive even in poorest soil.

## Cornus · Dogwood

**Florida.** See Deciduous Trees.
**Florida rubra.** See Deciduous Trees.
**Mascula.** Small yellow flowers in April, and beautiful, orange-colored berries in autumn.

*CORNUS, continued*

**Sanguinea** (Red Siberian Dogwood). Small white flower in May; the bright red bark in winter, even becoming brighter as the cold increases, adds much to the landscape.
**Stolonifera** (Red Osier Dogwood). White flowers; reddish purple bark in winter.

## Corylus

**Americana** (Filbert, or Hazelnut). See Nuts.
**Avellana purpurea** (Purple-leaved Hazelnut). Large shrub; bronzy purple leaves.

## Crataegus

**Crus-galli** (Cockspur Thorn). Spiny branches; white flowers in large clusters.
**Oxyacantha** (English Hawthorn). Single, white flowers, and scarlet fruits.

## Deutzia

**Candida.** White; tall.
**Crenata.** Double, pink; tall grower; very pretty.
**Gracilis.** Dwarf and compact; abundance of little white flowers.
**Lemoine.** White flowers.
**Pride of Rochester.** Double, pink-and-white flowers; tall.

Hydrangea paniculata grandiflora (see page 20)

## Euonymus

**Alatus** (Japanese Cork-barked Euonymus). A very interesting shrub, having singularly winged bark; leaves turn scarlet in autumn; berries red.
**Europæus.** A large-growing shrub, made very conspicuous in autumn and winter by its pinkish seed-pods, from which hang orange-colored berries.

## Exochorda

**Grandiflora** (Pearl Bush). White flowers in great abundance during May.

## Forsythia · Golden Bell

**Fortunei.** Very upright growth; produces bright yellow flowers early in April.
**Intermedia.** Good foliage; bright yellow flowers.
**Suspensa.** Of rather drooping habit; pretty, clear yellow flowers.
**Viridissima.** Very robust grower; greenish bark; foliage rich green.

## Halesia · Silver Bell

**Tetraptera** (Silver Bell). Pretty, white, bell-shaped flowers in May; grows tall.

## Hamamelis

**Virginica** (Witch Hazel). Bears small yellow flowers in late autumn.

## Hibiscus Syriacus

*Althaea, or Rose of Sharon*

**Ardens.** Double; purple.
**Boule de Feu.** Double; red.
**Cœlestis.** Purplish blue.
**Joan of Arc.** Double; white.
**Lady Stanley.** Double; white and red.
**Teas'.** Double; white.
**Totus albus.** Single; white.
**Totus rubrus.** Single; red.

## Hydrangea

**Arborescens grandiflora** (Hills of Snow). Showy white flowers in early summer, and lasting several weeks; very good foliage, not affected by heat or drought, and grows and blooms in shade where not too dense; very satisfactory.
**Hortensis, Otaksa.** A very useful variety. Atmosphere and soil seem to have muchyto do with the color of its flowers, which vary, being either pink or blue; near the sea they are inclined to be blue. They are not, generally speaking, hardy here and require protection; or, better yet, cultivate them in tubs or boxes and place in a cool cellar during winter, as the buds, being on the tips, are easily frozen off.
**Paniculata grandiflora.** The large cones of white flowers change to pink, after which they become purplish brown. These flowers last a long time, commencing in the late summer, and continuing several weeks. Can be grown as specimens, planted with other shrubs or grouped in clumps by themselves. They are very hardy and bloom in locations where many other shrubs fail.

Hydrangea Otaksa

Hedge of California Privet (Ligustrum ovalifolium)

## Hypericum

**Densiflorum.** Bears very pretty yellow flowers in July.

**Moserianum.** Of a low habit; has large, brilliant flowers and should be planted in a protected place.

## Jasminum

**Nudiflorum.** Bears yellow flowers very early in spring; has green bark; needs support for best effect, as the branches are of a drooping nature.

## Kerria

**Japonica.** Yellow flowers nearly all summer; bark is bright green.

## Laburnum · Golden Chain

A tall, slender-growing shrub, becoming really a small tree; yellow flowers, hanging in panicles, shaped very much like wistaria blossoms.

## Ligustrum · Privet

**Ovalifolium** (California Privet). While the primary use of this shrub is as a hedge plant, it is of much use as a specimen. We have it trimmed to globes, standards and large, compact bushes; some of very large dimensions. These plants are very valuable to give immediate effect in a new place; are excellent for the seashore, about railway stations and many places where other shrubs would be anything but thrifty.

**Variegatum** (Variegated-leaved Privet). While this makes a very nice border, it is also of much use as a foliage plant in the shrubbery, where it contrasts finely with plain-leaved shrubs.

*LIGUSTRUM, continued*

**Regelianum.** A very useful shrub, enduring in almost any reasonable soil or situation; is of more spreading habit than *L. ovalifolium*; also has white blossoms and blackish berries. An exceedingly valuable shrub for planting at the house foundations.

Lonicera Morrowi (see page 22)

## Lonicera · Bush Honeysuckle

**Fragrantissima.** Yellowish white flowers, having an elegant perfume, are borne in the very early spring. Of a spreading habit.
**Morrowi.** White flowers in May; pretty red berries in autumn.
**Tatarica alba.** Of upright habit; also has white flowers in May and red berries in fall.
**Tatarica rosea** (Pink Tartarian Honeysuckle). Very pretty when in bloom; bears red berries.
**Tatarica rubra.** Upright growth; red flowers.

## Pavia

**Macrostachya** (Bush Horse-Chestnut). Spikes of white flowers in summer.

## Philadelphus · Mock Orange

**Coronarius.** White flowers, which are very sweet.
**Coronarius aureus** (Golden-leaved Mock Orange). One of the best golden-leaved shrubs.
**grandiflorus.** Sweet-scented flowers; grows more rapidly than *P. coronarius*.

## Pyrus

**Japonica.** Red flowers in May.
**Umbellatica.** Pink flowers.

## Rhus

**Cotinus** (Smoke Bush). Large, loose plumes of purplish green bloom in June; tall.

## Ribes

**Aureum** (Yellow-flowering Currant). Bears flowers in April, which are of a delicious spicy fragrance, not found in any other blossom.
**Sanguineum** (Red-flowering Currant). Has red bark; bears clusters of ruddy purple flowers.

## Robinia

**Hispida.** Rose-colored flowers in May, which are borne in clusters much like wistaria.

## Rosa

**Rugosa.** Japanese single Rose, in pink and white varieties; large flowers during the early summer, and at intervals later, followed by red seed-pods; foliage is very robust and of a rich glossy green; very hardy; resists extremes of weather; also smoke and sea air fairly well.

## Sambucus

**Nigra aurea** (Golden-leaved Elder). White flowers in early summer; valued for its golden foliage.

## Spiraea

**Anthony Waterer.** One of the very best dwarf Spireas; blooms from June to October; flowers are crimson.
**Arguta.** Abundance of white flowers, entirely covering the branches, in early May; dwarf.
**Billardi.** Pretty pink flowers through the latter part of summer.
**Blue.** See *Caryopteris Mastacanthus*.
**Bumaldi.** Pink flowers all summer; dwarf and compact.
**Callosa alba.** Dwarf; white flowers all summer. Fine for planting in front of the higher-growing shrubs.
**Opulifolia aurea.** Pretty leaves in spring, of a decided golden hue, with small, pinkish white flowers appearing later; in autumn the foliage assumes beautiful tints; strong upright grower.
**Prunifolia** (Bridal Wreath). Small, double, white flowers in May, covering entire branches; grows tall and erect.

Spiræa Thunbergii (see page 23)

*SPIRAEA, continued*

**Reevesiana.** Very pretty clusters of white flowers in May; rather slow grower, becoming large when fully grown.

**Sorbifolia** (Ash-leaved Spirea). Very pretty, fern-like foliage, and plumes of white flowers in July; very distinct and striking.

**Thunbergii.** The earliest to bloom; has small, white flowers in abundance and pretty little leaves on graceful, drooping branches. One of the most conspicuous spring-flowering shrubs and fine for hedges.

**Van Houttei.** One of the very best. Grows tall but very easily kept within bounds; the pretty little flowers are borne in clusters and the plant, when in bloom, is entirely covered; foliage is good; the branches are drooping, giving the shrub a very graceful and handsome appearance in sprig.

## Stuartia

Makes a small tree of great merit; flowers are white, with purplish center, and of good size; midsummer.

## Stephanandra

**Flexuosa.** This dainty little shrub is planted chiefly for its foliage, which maintains a pretty green in the driest soil and during the hottest weather and gets pretty autumn colors; bears small, creamy white flowers in June.

## Styrax

**Japonica.** White, bell-shaped flowers ranged along the branches in May; tall.

*Spiræa Van Houttei*

## Symphoricarpos

**Racemosus** (Snowberry). Small pink flowers in May, followed by pearly white berries of fair size, which remain bright until very cold weather.

**Vulgaris** (Indian Currant). Red berries are borne in great profusion the entire length of branches and remain bright until after leaves fall.

## Syringa · Lilac

### SINGLE-FLOWERING VARIETIES

**Charles X.** Reddish purple.
**Gloire de Lorraine.** Mauve.
**Gloire de la Rochelle.** Light rose.
**Japonica.** Creamy white.
**Josikæa.** Purple.
**Louis Van Houtte.** Dark red.
**Persica.** Purple.
**Souvenir de Ludwig Spæth.** Dark purplish red.
**Villosa.** Light purple in bud; white when open.
**Vulgaris.** Common purple.
**Vulgaris alba.** Common white.
**Vulgaris, Congo.** Bright red.

### DOUBLE-FLOWERING VARIETIES

**Charles Joly.** Dark reddish purple.
**La Tour d'Auvergne.** Violet-purple.
**Madame Casimir Perier.** White.
**Madame Julius Finger.** Pink.
**Michael Buchner.** Pale lilac.
**Monument Carnot.** Lilac-blue.
**President Grevy.** Rosy violet.
**Prince de Beauveau.** Violet-rose.
**Pyramidalis.** Pale blue.
**Virginity.** Soft pink.

*Lilac, Marie Legraye (see page 24)*

## DECIDUOUS SHRUBS — JAMES KREWSON & SONS

### Syringa, Standard or Tree Form
**Alphonse Lavalle.** Double; bluish lilac.
**Charles X.** Single; reddish purple.
**Colmariensis.** Single; pale blue.
**Dr. Breitschneider.** Double; purplish in bud, opening white.
**Dr. Masters.** Double; lilac.
**Dr. Troyanowsky.** Double; mauve.
**Edouard Andre.** Double; rose.
**Frau Dammann.** Single; white.
**Lamarck.** Double; rosy lilac.
**Leon Simon.** Double; bluish crimson.
**Lilarosa.** Single; silvery pink.
**Louis Van Houtte.** Single; dark red.
**Madame Abel Chatenay.** Double; pure white.
**Madame Lemoine.** Double; white.
**Marc Michæli.** Double; lilac-blue.
**Marie Legraye.** Single; white. One of the handsomest white Lilacs.
**Othello.** Single; dark purplish red.
**Philemon.** Single; dark reddish purple.
**President Grevy.** Double; rosy violet.
**President Loubet.** Double; purplish red.
**President Viger.** Double; bluish lilac.
**Princess Alexandra.** Single; white.
**Souvenir de Ludwig Spæth.** Single; dark purplish red.
**Toussaint l'Ouverture.** Single; purple.
**Villosa.** Single; light purple in bud, white when open.
**Viviand Morel.** Single; light bluish lilac with white center.
**William Robinson.** Single; violet-mauve.

### Tamarix · Tamarisk
A pleasing shrub of slender growth; a very quick grower and is very much improved by severe pruning annually; the feathery foliage and the plumes of pink, feathery blossoms make a nice effect.

### Viburnum
**Dentatum** (Arrowwood). White flowers in May, followed by crimson fruit, which changes to black.
**Lantana** (Wayfaring Tree). White flowers in May, red fruit in autumn.
**Opulus** (High-bush Cranberry). An exceedingly ornamental shrub, with flat crowns of white flowers in June and large red berries in autumn.
**Opulus sterilis** (The Old-fashioned Snowball). Large, round, white "snowballs" gracefully hanging in groups at the ends of the branches.
**Plicatum** (Japan Snowball). White flowers, set in pairs, are dotted evenly the entire length of the branches, changing from greenish white to the purest white; remains in blossom a long time; foliage is rich green. This shrub is of great value and does well in almost any situation.
**Tomentosum.** White flowers in May and scarlet berries in autumn; noted for its elegant, compact shape and rich green foliage, which colors beautifully after frost.

### Weigela
A group of shrubs that should be more generally planted. They are free bloomers, have no insect enemies, and thrive in almost any soil.

**Candida.** White flowers in June.
**Eva Rathke.** Deep carmine-red flowers, from early June to frost; foliage turns rich shades of reddish bronze in autumn.
**Floribunda.** Red flowers; rapid grower.
**Nivea.** White flowers in June and at intervals later; excellent foliage.
**Rosea.** A variety of much merit, having a wealth of rosy pink flowers in June.
**Van Houttei.** Carmine flowers; June.
**Variegata.** Pink flowers in May; variegated foliage, remaining a good color until frost.

Weigela rosea

---

We exercise the greatest care in the growing of our evergreens, and deliver them with a solid ball of earth wrapped in burlap. They are sure to live if given the slightest attention.

## Roses

We make a specialty of potted and Standard or Tree Roses. We have a good list of Everblooming and Tea Roses, and give particular attention to potted plants, which can be planted out at any time of year, when the ground is not frozen; they are already started and often in bloom. The Standard or Tree Roses are very ornamental, adding much pleasure the entire summer.

### Monthly, or Everblooming

**Caroline Testout.** Pink.
**Clothilde Soupert.** Rose.
**Etoile de Lyon.** Yellow.
**Gruss an Teplitz.** Crimson.
**Hermosa.** Pink.
**Jonkheer J. L. Mock.** Carmine.
**Kaiserin Augusta Victoria.** White.
**Killarney.** Pink and white.
**La Detroit.** Dark rose.
**La France.** Pink and white.
**Madame Jules Grolez.** Rose.
**Madame Ravary.** Yellow.
**Maman Cochet.** Deep rose-pink; good grower.
**Marie Van Houtte.** Creamy white, rose margin.
**Meteor.** Crimson.
**Mevrouw G. W. Van Gelderen.** Creamy rose.
**Mrs. B. R. Cant.** Red.
**My Maryland.** Salmon-pink.
**Wm. R. Smith.** Creamy white, with shadings of rose.

Mrs. John Laing Rose (see page 26)

Visit our Nurseries and see the things in actual growth before you buy them.

## Hybrid Perpetual Roses

**Anna de Diesbach.** Carmine.
**Baronne de Rothschild.** Light pink.
**Frau Karl Druschki.** White.
**General Jacqueminot.** Scarlet.
**Hugh Dickson.** Crimson.
**Madame Gabriel Luizet.** Pink.
**Magna Charta.** Pink.
**Margaret Dickson.** White.
**Mrs. John Laing.** Pink.
**Paul Neyron.** Dark rose.

## Standard or Tree Roses

**Caroline Testout.** Pink.
**Flower of Fairfield.** Crimson.
**Frau Karl Druschki.** White.

STANDARD OR TREE ROSES, continued

**Gruss an Teplitz.** Crimson.
**Kaiserin Augusta Victoria.** White.
**Killarney.** Pink and White.
**Madame Norbert Levavasseur.** Crimson.
**Madame Ravery.** Yellow.
**Magna Charta.** Pink.
**Mevrouw G. W. Van Gelderen.** Creamy rose

## Dwarf Polyantha Roses

**Baby Dorothy** (Madame Levavasseur). Pink.
**Katherine Zeimet.** White.
**Madame Norbert Levavasseur.** Crimson.
**Mrs. W. Cutbush.** Pink.

RAMBLER ROSES. See Vines

# Weeping and Formal Trees and Shrubs

## Acer

**Platanoides globosa** (Globe Norway Maple). A new formal tree.

## Buxus · Box

We have a fine collection of these in standard, globe, obelisk and square forms.

Teas' Weeping Mulberry

## Catalpa

**Bungei** (Umbrella Tree). A very popular and much admired formal tree; has very large, healthy-looking foliage.

## Cerasus

**Rosea pendula** (Japanese Weeping Rose-flowering Cherry). The abundant, beautiful pink bloom can be seen as far as the eye can reach; the tree also has good foliage.

## Fagus

**Sylvatica pendula** (Weeping Beech). A very interesting tree of large growth.

## Ligustrum

**Ovalifolium** (California Privet). We have hundreds of formal Privets; standard forms are one of our specialties.

## Morus

**Alba pendula** (Tea's Weeping Mulberry). One of the best drooping trees; always green and bright throughout the driest weather; holds its leaves until late.

## Roses

We make Standard Roses one of our specialties, having many varieties.

## Ulmus

**Montana pendula** (Camperdown Weeping Elm). One of the most picturesque drooping trees; is of larger growth than the Weeping Mulberry.

## Picea

**Excelsa pendula** (Weeping Norway Spruce). If allowed its freedom, will grow into a variety of shapes, no two specimens being alike.

# Vines

*Clematis paniculata*

### Akebia
**Quinata.** Clover-like leaves; curious, purple, waxy flowers; always neat and pretty.

### Ampelopsis
**Veitchii** (Japanese or Boston Ivy). The popular vine for covering walls, etc. Leaves turn very beautiful in autumn.

### Aristolochia
**Sipho** (Dutchman's Pipe). Heart-shaped, dark green leaves; curious, yellowish, pipe-shaped flowers.

### Bignonia
**Grandiflora** (Chinese Trumpet Flower). Fine, large, orange-scarlet flowers, late summer until frost; very showy.
**Radicans** (Old-fashioned Trumpet Vine). We have these from small plants up to large specimens, grown on poles for immediate effect.

### Celastrus
**Scandens** (Bittersweet). Rapid grower; beautiful crimson seeds in late autumn.

### Clematis
**Henryi.** White; large flower.
**Jackmanii.** Rich blue; large flower.
**Mme. Edouard Andre.** Red; large flower.
**Mme. Baron Veillard.** Pink; large flower.
**Paniculata** (Japanese Clematis). White, feathery flowers in August; very rapid grower.

### Hedera
**Helix** (English Ivy). One of the best evergreen Ivies. We have a nice stock, pot-grown.

### Lonicera · Honeysuckle
We offer several varieties of the pot-grown plants.

### Lycium
**Chinense** (Chinese Matrimony Vine). A rapid-growing vine, with thorns; bears pretty red berries.

### Pueraria
**Thunbergii** (Kudzu Vine). Large leaves; one of the most rapid-growing vines known.

### Roses, Climbing
**Crimson Rambler.** Bright crimson; in clusters.
**Dorothy Perkins.** Pink; excellent foliage.
**Flower of Fairfield.** Crimson.
**Lady Gay.** Pink; very nice foliage.
**Tausendschon.** Pink, changing to carmine when open; light center; flowers large, single.
**White Dorothy Perkins.**
**Yellow Rambler.**

Lonicera (Honeysuckle)

## Vinca

**Minor** (Myrtle, or Periwinkle). Fine for covering or on rockeries; grows in shade.

## Wistaria

We offer a very large selection of Wistarias in various sizes, from small vines to very large specimens, grown on poles, some of which are 10 or more feet high. These vines are very much desired for covering pergolas, dead trees or any purpose for which immediate effect is desired. Wistarias are very slow to burst out in leaf after planting; sometimes they do not show signs of leaves the first season until midsummer; severe pruning and plenty of water will assist them very much to get a start. We have, also, plenty of Wistarias trained to standards or trees.

**Alba.** White.
**Chinensis.** Beautiful blue.
**Frutescens.** Rich purple; blooms late.

## Hardy Grasses and Reeds

**ARUNDO Donax.** A very tall Bamboo, growing 10 to 12 feet high; has long, drooping, light green foliage and pretty plumes.

**ERIANTHUS Ravennæ.** A tall, neat-growing, green Grass; sturdy and bears pretty silvery plumes. Very effective and hardy. Grows about 6 feet high.

**EULALIA gracillima.** A rich green, robust Grass; very graceful, with its pretty plumes. Grows about 5 feet high.

**Japonica.** Has broad, dark green leaves; about 6 feet high.

**Japonica variegata.** A pretty Grass, with green and yellow stripes, also very nice plumes; 4 feet high.

Crimson Rambler Rose (see page 27)

**Eulalia Japonica zebrina.** Green, with yellow spots dotted along the leaves; grows about 5 feet high.

**PHALARIS** (Ribbon Grass). Two varieties. One has golden and green stripes; the other, silver and green stripes; both are used as a border to Grass beds and grow 2 to 3 feet high.

Bed of Ornamental Grasses

Planting of Herbaceous Plants

## Herbaceous Plants

We give more attention each year to hardy garden plants, and take much pleasure in laying out hardy gardens and borders. By growing larger quantities and adding new varieties, our stock is constantly increasing, and at present we have many of these varieties in large clumps, several years old, for immediate effect. The average height is given, but will vary much according to soil, and time of flowering will vary with seasons and locations.

**ACHILLEA, The Pearl.** Blooms nearly all summer; very nice to cut; white; 2 ft.

**AGROSTEMMA Coronaria.** Rose; 2 ft.; June, July.

**ALYSSUM saxatile compactum.** Yellow; 12 in.; early May.

**ANTHEMIS tinctoria.** Yellow; 18 in.; July, August.

**AQUILEGIA** (Columbine). Very pretty flowers and foliage, the flowers lasting several weeks; will thrive in any soil. Assorted colors; 2 ft.; May, June.

**ASTERS.** These are excellent for the background, on account of their height, which is about 4 ft.; bloom late in September and last quite a long time.

**ASTILBE Japonica** (Herbaceous Spirea). White plumes of flowers; pretty foliage; 12 in.; May.

**BOLTONIA asteroides.** Tall stems, 5 ft. high; produce immense numbers of miniature, white, daisy-like flowers; August, September.

**CAMPANULA** (Canterbury Bells). Assorted colors; 2 ft.; June.

Aquilegia (Columbine)

CASSIA Marylandica. This is very gorgeous when in bloom, with its large panicles of yellow flowers, spotted with brownish red. The foliage is very pretty, resembling that of the locust; 4 ft.; late July.
CHRYSANTHEMUM. An almost indispensable flower, as it appears when everything else in the garden is gone, giving cheer and color for a long period. We usually have about fifteen or twenty of the many varieties, in bronze, pink, red, yellow, etc.
CONVALLARIA (Lily-of-the-Valley). Wands of dainty white, fragrant bell-shaped flowers. We have strong clumps for immediate effect. They like a moist, shady situation.
COREOPSIS lanceolata grandiflora. Very popular; rich, yellow, daisy-like flowers on long stems, making it very useful for cutting; very easy of cultivation; blooms in late June or early July.
DELPHINIUM Chinense (Larkspur). Blue; 2 ft.
  Formosum. Very robust; rich blue; 3 ft.
DIANTHUS. Old-fashioned Pinks; 1 ft.; May.
  Barbatus (Sweet William). Grand variety of colors and shadings; very nice for cutting; 18 in.; June.
DIELYTRA spectabilis (Bleeding Heart). Beautiful sprays of pink, heart-shaped flowers in May; 12 in.

Delphinium (Larkspur)

DIGITALIS (Foxglove). We offer some strong clumps, of a variety of colors; 3 ft.; midsummer.
FUNKIA (Plantain Lily).
  Cærulea. Blue; 2 ft.; August.
  Subcordata alba. White; 2 ft.; August.
  Variegata. Lavender flowers and pretty green-and-white leaves; fine border plant; dwarf; August.
GAILLARDIA. An excellent plant for cutting; flowers are orange, with dark red center; 2 ft.; summer.
HELIANTHUS (Hardy Sunflower). Single and double varieties; very pretty yellow flowers. August, September.
  Soleil d'Or. Double; yellow; 2 to 3 ft.; August, September.
HEMEROCALLIS fulva (Orange Day Lily). Rich yellow; 4 ft.; July.
HIBISCUS (Mallow). Beautiful plant, with large, open, pink flowers, with purple center; very showy; 4 ft.; August.
HIERACIUM (Tawny Hawkweed). Orange and red; thrives in any soil; June to October.
HOLLYHOCKS. Pink, red, white and yellow; 5 to 6 ft.; July, August.
IBERIS (Candytuft). White flowers in handsome clusters; 12 in.; April. Fine for borders.

Helianthus (Hardy Sunflower)

Iris Kaempferi (Japanese Iris)

## IRIS

### IRIS GERMANICA (German Iris)
*Late May*

**Canariense.** Light yellow.
**Edith.** Light plumbago-blue and purple.
**Honorabilis.** Yellow and bronze.
**Julius Cæsar.** Yellow and bronze.
**L'Avenir.** Lavender and white.
**Madame Chereau.** White, richly veined with purple; sweet.
**Nana.** Yellow and brown.

### IRIS KAEMPFERI (Japanese Iris)
We have a collection of large, blooming clumps of Japan Iris, in about twenty varieties, some having three and others six petals. They are a grand sight when in bloom; June, July.
**Gekko-No-Nami.** Early white.
**Hallock.** Violet; pretty curled petals; very double.
**Hannibal.** Rich purple veins on white ground; six petals.
**Mahogany.** Deep red, yellow center; six petals.
**Orion.** White, margin purple; fine; six petals.
**Robert Christy.** Pink veins on light rose ground.
**No. 15.** Large; white; three petals.
**No. 16.** Silvery white, overlaid with violet; three petals.
**No. 23.** Lilac, white veins; three petals.
**No. 43.** White, violet veins; three petals.
**No. 67.** White; late-flowering; three petals.
**No. 72.** Rich blue; six petals.
**No. 73.** Silvery white; three petals.
**No. 79.** Rosy pink; three petals.
**No. 82.** Purple, white spots; three petals.

**IRIS orientalis.** Blue with bronze markings; May.
**Sibirica.** Rich blue; tall; profuse bloomer; early June.
**LOBELIA cardinalis.** Bright crimson; 2 ft.; August.
**LYSIMACHIA clethroides** (Loosestrife). White spikes; 2 ft.; July, August.
**LYCHNIS Chalcedonica** (Lamp Flower). Has bright scarlet flowers; 2 ft.; July.
**MONTBRETIA.** Orange suffused with red; August.
**MYOSOTIS** (Forget-me-not). May to September.
**NARCISSUS.** White; sweet-scented; April.

### Paeonia

**Bicolor.** Light rose, yellowish center.
**Brennus.** Double; crimson.
**Cleopatra.** Large; rosy pink, yellow center; single.
**Delachei.** Purplish red.
**Festiva maxima.** Large; white, crimson spots in center; fine.
**Fragrans.** A great bloomer; large, double, rich pink flowers are borne in great profusion, on long stems.
**Francois Ortegat.** Rich purple; fine.
**Grandiflora rubra.** Large; double; red; late.
**Hercules.** Large, single flowers; velvety crimson, yellow center.

Pæonia officinalis rubra (see page 32)

## PERENNIALS

*Perennial Phlox*

### Paeonia, continued

**Humei rosea.** Large, double flowers; rich pink; sweet-scented; late.
**L'Esperance.** Pink; beautiful flower and bud; fragrant, very pleasing, fine; early.
**Mutabilis alba.** Blush-white; semi-double; early.
**Officinalis rubra.** Rich, velvety crimson; double; early.
**Phormis.** Wine-red; double.
**Pulcherrima.** Purplish pink.
**Queen Victoria.** Fine creamy white; early.
**Reevesiana.** Fine reddish pink; late.
**Sinensis rubra.** Reddish pink; late.
**Solfatare.** Rich yellowish white; double.
**Triomphe du Nord.** Large; light rose and pink.
**PENTSTEMON barbatus.** Scarlet spikes; all midsummer; 3 ft.

### Phlox decussata

We are constantly adding new varieties to our list of Phloxes, and always have a good selection of colors. Have many varieties not enumerated here.

**Bacchante.** Rich, rosy purple, dark eye.
**Bridesmaid.** White, crimson eye.
**Coquelicot.** Bright crimson.
**Eclaireur.** Carmine-purple; large flowers.
**Elizabeth Campbell.** Rosy pink.
**Etna.** Salmon-red.
**Eugene Danzenvillier.** Lilac, white margin.
**H. O. Wijers.** White, crimson eye.
**Jeanne d'Arc.** Good white.
**King of the Purples.** Fine purple.
**La Vague.** Mauve, with aniline red eye.
**Levavasseur.** White center, rosy pink margin.

### Phlox decussata, continued

**Mozart.** White, carmine center; large flowers.
**Pearl.** A fine, robust white.
**R. P. Struthers.** Rosy carmine, red eye; fine.
**PHLOX subulata rosea** (Mountain Pink). A very pretty creeping plant, which succeeds almost anywhere, in shade, out in the open, or on rockeries; pink; 6 in.; April.
**PLATYCODON** (Chinese Bellflower). Blue or white; 2 ft.; July to September.
**PRIMULA veris** (Cowslip). Many colors; 6 to 8 ft.; April.
  **Vulgaris** (English Primrose). Yellow flowers; dark green leaves; 6 in.; April.
**PYRETHRUM roseum.** Pretty pink, daisy-like flowers on long stems; fine for cutting; 2 ft.; May, June.
**RUDBECKIA** (Golden Glow). Double yellow flowers; 5 ft.; July to September.
**SEDUM acre.** A very low-growing, creeping plant, with small yellow flowers; 4 in.
  **Kamtschaticum.** Yellow flowers, green leaves, which turn rich red in winter; 6 in.; May.
  **Spectabile** (Giant Stonecrop). Very showy pink flowers; 18 to 24 in.; September.
**STOKESIA cyanea** (Cornflower Aster). Double blue flowers; 18 to 24 in.; June to October.
**TRADESCANTIA** (Spiderwort). Blue flowers.
**TRITOMA** (Red-hot Poker). Pretty orange and red spikes; 3 ft.; August, September.
**VERONICA spicata.** Rich blue spikes; 2 ft.; July to September.
  **subsessilis** (Bluebird Flower). Pretty blue spikes; 2 ft.; July.
**YUCCA** (Adam's Needle). Evergreen leaves, white lily-like flowers borne on long stems; 4 to 5 ft.; June, July.

*Primula veris*

CHELTENHAM, PENNSYLVANIA                              FRUIT TREES    33

## Fruit Department

The time of ripening given to fruits listed in this catalogue may differ with others, but these dates apply to this immediate section, and will differ with seasons, also.

### Apples

Apples must receive more attention in this locality; during the past few years the ravages of the scale and time have carried off nearly all the grand old trees, and unless we come to the rescue, we will miss our annual treat of the beautiful Apple blossoms and ripe fruit.

The scale seems to be about vanquished, and with a little care, together with a proper selection of varieties, adapted to one's particular purpose or location, will prove a profitable investment, whether a single tree or an orchard is planted.

#### SUMMER VARIETIES

**Early Harvest.** Yellow when fully ripened; mellow, rich and pleasing; bears abundantly when young; makes a shapely, medium-sized tree. Early August.

Grimes' Golden Apple (see page 34)

Stark Apple

## SUMMER APPLES, continued

**Red Astrachan.** Nearly covered with crimson, excepting a small patch on one side; flesh is white, crisp and of excellent flavor, making a good cooking or an attractive eating Apple; bears when very young. August.

**Williams' Early.** A nice, early, red Apple, of excellent color and quality; tree grows upright and handsome; very desirable. August.

**Yellow Transparent.** This is one of the earliest Apples under cultivation; tree bears when but a few years old; fruit is of good size, color and quality, and as it ripens, makes a very pretty sight among the large, dark green foliage, for which this variety is noted.

## AUTUMN AND WINTER VARIETIES

**Baldwin.** Large, bright red, slightly acid, juicy and rich; bears when young and makes a very symmetrical tree. Fruit ripens in this locality October and November.

**Ben Davis.** Greenish yellow, red-striped; very productive; bears very abundantly when young. November, December.

**Cornell's Favorite.** Red, large, handsome, good flavor; bears abundantly when very young; makes a handsome tree. Early September.

**Fall Pippin.** Yellow, rich-flavored and of medium size. November.

**Fallawater.** A favorite eating Apple; greenish yellow, with slight blush; large and sweet; very productive. November.

## AUTUMN AND WINTER APPLES, con

**Fameuse** (Snow Apple). Glossy red, medium size, handsome; flesh is snow-white, rich, juicy, mellow and very pleasing. October, November.

**Gravenstein.** A very productive, small-growing tree; fruit is of medium size, greenish, heavily streaked with red; acid. September.

**Grimes' Golden.** Of medium size, yellow, tender, crisp, juicy and delicious. A winter Apple of much value for this locality, keeping, under proper care, until late April.

**King.** An excellent Apple of large size, yellow striped with red and of delicious flavor. November, December.

**Maiden's Blush.** The "Blush Apple" is known by everybody as a valuable general-purpose Apple; yellow with red cheek; grows to be a large tree. September.

**McIntosh Red.** Very much like the Fameuse, only larger and a longer keeper. December.

**Northern Spy.** Large; greenish yellow streaked with red; flesh yellow and firm; has a very pleasing acid flavor; very productive and is somewhat inclined to rot some seasons. October, November.

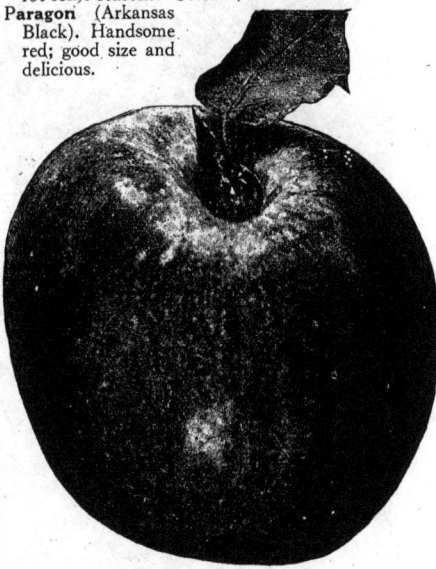

**Paragon** (Arkansas Black). Handsome red; good size and delicious.

York Imperial Apple

# CHELTENHAM, PENNSYLVANIA — FRUIT TREES

## AUTUMN AND WINTER APPLES, continued

**Rome Beauty.** A large, delicious fall Apple; of a beautiful color; mellow and highly pleasing. October.

**Smith's Cider.** The old-fashioned Cider Apple. Winter.

**Smokehouse.** An old favorite; of large size; yellow; firm and rich. November.

**Stark.** Large; greenish yellow, heavily streaked with red; a very good winter Apple. Late winter.

**Stayman's Winesap.** Rich red; medium size; good bearer; very hardy and vigorous; an excellent winter Apple. December.

**Talman's Sweet.** Yellow with blush on side; rich and sweet. Winter.

**Wealthy.** Above average size; heavily streaked with red; very productive. December, January.

**York Imperial.** An Apple that originated in York County, Pa.; whitish shaded with crimson; firm and of good flavor; one of the very best winter Apples for this section. December.

## CRAB APPLES

**Red Siberian.** A good one; very productive, and a pretty-shaped tree; fruit bright red.

**Transcendent.** Yellow, heavily streaked with crimson; pretty blossoms; larger and more spreading habit than Red Siberian.

## DWARF APPLES

Baldwin — Northern Spy.
Fameuse. — Yellow Transparent.

## Apricots

We recommend planting Apricots in a northern exposure. They are a delicious fruit and have pretty blossoms. We offer several varieties.

## Cherries

### SWEET VARIETIES

**Black Tartarian.** Large; dark; very rich and a good keeper. A very popular Cherry.

**Centennial.** Light red; good size.

**Governor Wood.** Yellow, bright red cheek; tender, juicy, sweet and delicious; bears when very young.

**Late Duke.** Red; acid; large size; bears when very young. Makes a shapely tree of medium size.

**May Duke.** Red when fully ripe; good size.

**Napoleon.** The old-fashioned solid Oxheart. Yellow with red cheek; large. Tree grows very large and spreading.

**Windsor.** Dark red; firm, and a good keeper; large. Bears when young.

**Yellow Spanish.** Yellowish white, slight blush; sweet and juicy.

### SOUR VARIETIES

**Dyehouse.** Bright red; acid; juicy; very early. Bears when young.

**Early Richmond.** Bright red; acid; large; ripens early. Tree grows to fair size and is very productive.

**Montmorency.** Large, handsome red fruit, ripening late; very productive and profitable; bears when very young. Succeeds everywhere.

## Mulberries, Russian

## Nectarines

## Peaches

**Alexander.** A very early Peach of medium size; greenish yellow, with a blush on one side. Early to middle of July.

**Beer's Smock.** One of the richest yellow Peaches; flesh highly colored and delicious. Late.

**Belle of Georgia.** White, with red cheek; flesh white and firm; a very good, profitable variety of large size. Late July.

**Bilyeu's October.** White, with blush on side. Very late.

**Carman.** Yellowish white, red blush; flesh white; good size. Late July.

Black Tartarian Cherries

Basket of Peaches

### PEACHES, continued

**Chair's Choice.** Yellow, red cheek; splendid flavor and large size. Late.

**Champion.** A large white Peach, red around the stone; flesh white and juicy. Tree is a strong grower. Early August.

**Crawford Early.** Yellow, with blush on side; of excellent flavor; productive and hardy. Middle of August.

**Crawford Late.** This Peach ripens about September 10 to 15; yellow, very large, rich and of highest quality. Tree grows to a good size and lives to be very old.

**Crosby.** A medium-sized Peach, ripening about September 1 to 10. Yellow with a red cheek.

**Elberta.** The great cropper. Yellow, with good coloring on cheek; rich, solid and of large size. A medium-sized tree when fully grown, but always bears enormous crops; in fact, it is advisable to thin the fruit early in the season. About September 1.

**Ford's Late.** White; very abundant bearer, often has to be thinned when Peaches are small to get best results. Late September.

**Foster.** Yellow, with red cheek; of good size. August.

**Fox's Seedling.** Very productive; yellow and of delicious flavor. This Peach is an excellent one for this section, having borne fruit when others were caught by late frosts, or buds destroyed by severe winters. September.

**Greensboro.** White, red cheek. An old and well-known favorite. Early.

**Morris White.** Another old favorite. Ripens middle of September.

**Mountain Rose.** A Peach of great merit, having a beautiful red blush nearly covering it; has a delicious flavor; an abundant bearer and very hardy. Late July.

Elberta Peaches

Bartlett Pears

#### PEACHES, continued

**Oldmixon.** Excellent flavor; creamy white with blush; is an old favorite. Ripens about September 1 to 10.

**Reeves' Favorite.** Yellow, red cheek; excellent quality; large. Middle of September.

**Salway.** A very late yellow Peach; flavor good.

**Sneed.** White; very early; freestone; good flavor. A good early Peach.

**Stump the World.** One of the best-flavored; white with a red cheek; very rich and juicy. Ripens in early to middle September.

**Susquehanna.** Yellow, red cheek. Ripens about September 1 to 10.

**Triumph.** Yellow, with blush on side. Ripens about the middle of July.

## Pears

**Bartlett.** Large, rich and juicy. Well known by all. Early September.

**Beurre d'Anjou.** A very large, greenish yellow Pear of excellent flavor. October.

**Beurre Gifford.** A fine-flavored Pear of medium size; good color when ripe. Late August.

**Clapp's Favorite.** Very large; yellow with red blush, excellent flavor; should be ripened indoors; bears when young. August, September.

**Doyenne d'Ete.** A very early Pear; small but of good flavor; bears when young. July.

**Kieffer.** Vigorous, hardy, very productive and profitable; better results are obtained if fruit is thinned while small. October, November.

**Lawrence.** Medium size, very sweet and juicy, handsome yellow when fully ripe; bears when quite young and is very productive. October, November.

#### PEARS, continued

**Le Conte.** A very abundant and sure bearer, robust grower; has handsome, large, dark green leaves; the fruit is best ripened indoors and is of good quality; a much-desired canning and preserving Pear, being of good size and shape. We have trees bearing here that have not missed a large crop in years. September.

**Manning's Elizabeth.** A very pretty, compact-growing tree; the fruit is small, beautifully colored and delicious; very prolific. August.

**Pres. Drouard.** A greenish yellow Pear of good size; very productive and good when properly ripened. Late autumn.

**Seckel.** The tree is a slow, compact grower, of very handsome and symmetrical shape; bears when young. There is hardly a Pear with better flavor than this popular variety. October.

**Sheldon.** A large, round, russet-colored Pear of fine flavor; very productive and profitable. September.

**Tyson.** Originated in this vicinity; upright grower; fruit large and rich in flavor; of its season it is one of the best. September 1.

**Wilder's Early.** A small-growing, rather irregular tree, bearing very highly colored, delicious fruit; yellow, with the brightest red coloring. August.

### DWARF VARIETIES

**Duchess.** A large, fine-flavored Pear, very juicy and good both for dessert and canning.

We have also the following varieties in dwarf form, described in the following list:

| Bartlett. | Seckel. | Tyson. |
| Clapp's Favorite. | Wilder's Early. |

---

Our list of Fruits is not large, but every tree and plant is a gem

## Plums

**Abundance.** A Japanese variety; upright grower; good bearer; red. Early.
**Burbank.** A good Japan Plum of more spreading growth than Abundance and ripens later.
**German Prune.** Large and oblong; purplish blue, with yellow flesh; sweet.
**Imperial Gage.** Greenish yellow; good size.
**Red June.** An early red sort; good flavor; upright, vigorous grower.
**Shipper's Pride.** Large, round and of a blue color; a good cropper.
**Shropshire Damson.** A small blue Plum, always in great demand; a much-desired preserving variety; tree is a good, vigorous grower.

## Quinces

**Bourgeat.** A rapid, upright grower; fruit large.
**Champion.** Light greenish yellow; large size; good variety and very productive.
**Orange.** Deep golden yellow; medium size; rich and productive.
**Rea's Mammoth.** Large, pear-shaped; good and productive.

## Small Fruits

### Grapes

**Brighton.** Rather small berries, very sweet and red.
**Campbell's Early.** Very large, solid, blue berries; excellent keeper.
**Catawba.** Red, very sweet and of good size.
**Concord.** The most extensively planted Grape in this section; dark blue, very sweet, productive, vigorous and hardy; an excellent Grape for all purposes.
**Delaware.** Delicious; small, compact bunches; red.
**Moore's Early.** Very early; black; good, compact bunches.
**Niagara.** The best white Grape for this section; vigorous grower, hardy and very productive; has large bunches of big berries, which are of excellent flavor.
**Salem.** Berries very large and red, with thick skin; strong grower.
**Worden.** Similar to Concord, but somewhat earlier; very sweet, uniform and productive.

### Currants

**Black Naples.** Good size; black.
**Cherry.** Very large and bright red.
**Fay's Prolific.** An excellent red Currant.
**La Versailles.** A good, strong, vigorous-growing, red Currant.
**White Grape.** A good white variety.

*Burbank Plums*

### Gooseberries

**Downing.** Of good size; greenish color; very sturdy, upright, strong bush.
**Houghton's Seedling.** Red when fully ripe; very abundant bearer.

### Blackberries

**Eldorado.** Vigorous and productive; large berries.
**Wilson.** Large berries; a good productive variety.

### Raspberries

**Cumberland.** One of the largest Blackcaps.
**Cuthbert.** An old and very popular red Raspberry; good flavor, productive and hardy.
**Golden Queen.** The favorite yellow variety.
**Marlboro.** A good dark red variety.
**St. Regis.** The new everbearing red Raspberry.

### Nuts

**Black Walnut.** We offer various sizes of these.
**English Walnut.** These nuts are a great favorite and can easily be grown, if the tree is given a protected position; is more successfully planted in the early spring.
**Filbert** (Hazelnut). We recommend these bushes very highly, as being entirely hardy and very productive, seldom failing a crop, and without insect pests.
**Shellbark.** We offer small trees, the best size to plant, as it is difficult to get a large Shellbark tree to grow.

CHELTENHAM, PENNSYLVANIA TABLE OF INFORMATION 39

# Table of Information

Table of information concerning Shrubs, Deciduous and Evergreen—approximate height they attain, average time of flowering and color of flowers, together with special notes of habits and foliage. For additional descriptions, see under Shrubs.

| Time of Flowering | Common Name | Botanical Name | Color of Flowers | Height | Remarks |
|---|---|---|---|---|---|
| Midsummer | Rose of Sharon | Althæa | Assorted | 6–8 ft. | Handsome; erect growth. Blooms when flowers are not plentiful. |
| Late April | Juneberry | Amelanchier Canadensis | White | 4 ft. | Dark purple berries in July. |
| June | False Indigo | Amorpha fruticosa | Purple | 5–7 ft. | Long flower-spikes; strong grower. |
| May | Flg. Almond | Amygdalis | Pink and white | 3–4 ft. | Very pretty; slow grower. |
| Early April | | Andromeda | White | 2–3 ft. | Evergreen; flowers resemble lily-of-the-valley. |
| May | | Azalea amœna | Magenta | 3–4 ft. | Evergreen. Bloom covers entire plant. |
| April | | Azalea mollis and Pontica | Assorted | 3–4 ft. | Very gorgeous bloom. |
| September | Groundsel Shrub | Baccharis halimifolia | Snow-white | | Very showy. Succeeds best in well-drained situation. |
| Early April | Spice Bush | Benzoin | Yellow | 6–8 ft. | Flowers appear in spring before the leaves. In autumn very attractive with red berries. |
| | Barberry | Berberis | | | Noted for display of red berries all winter. |
| Late summer | | Buddleia Veitchii | Lilac | 4–5 ft. | Beautiful spikes of sweet-scented flowers. |
| July | Beauty Fruit | Callicarpa purpurea | Purple | 3–4 ft. | Showy berries during fall. |
| May | Sweet Shrub | Calycanthus | Brown | 5–7 ft. | Old-fashioned sweet-scented "Shrub." |
| May | Siberian Pea | Caragana arborescens | Yellow | Tall | |
| Aug. and Sept. | Blue Spirea | Caryopteris mastacanthus | Blue | 3–4 ft. | Rich blue flowers in profusion; very showy. |
| July | Wild Senna | Cassia Marylandica | Yellow | 4–5 ft. | Will thrive in any soil. |
| June | New Jersey Tea | Ceanothus Americanus | White | 3–4 ft. | Very ornamental. |
| July | Button Bush | Cephalanthus occidentalis. | White | Tall | |
| Early spring | Japan Judas | Cercis Japonica | Pink | | Branches covered with small flowers, before leaves appear in spring. Beautiful, glossy foliage. |
| June | White Fringe | Chionanthus Virginica | | Tall | Large leaves; purple fruit. Very desirable. |
| Early spring | Hardy Japan Orange | Citrus trifoliata | White | 6–8 ft. | Fragrant white flowers; orange-like fruit, not edible. |
| Early summer | Sweet Pepper | Clethra alnifolia | White | 4–5 ft. | Deliciously fragrant. |
| July | Bladder Senna | Colutea arborescens | Yellow | 6–8 ft. | Curious bladder-like seed-pods. |
| April | White Dogwood | Cornus florida | White | Tall | Beautiful red berries. |
| April | Pink Dogwood | Cornus florida rubra | Pink | Tall | Beautiful red berries; slower grower than the Florida. |
| April | Cornelian Cherry | Cornus mascula | Yellow | Tall | Beautiful red berries. |
| Late spring | Hawthorn | Cratægus | Red, pink and white | Tall | Pretty scarlet berries in autumn. |
| May, June | | Deutzia | Pink and white | | See Shrubs for description. |
| May | | Elæagnus longipes and umbellata | Yellow | 6–8 ft. | |
| | Cork-bark Euonymus | Euonymus alatus | | 4–6 ft. | Flowers very small; foliage turns bright red in fall; red berries. |
| | Strawberry Tree | Euonymus Europæus | | Tall | Beautiful orange-scarlet fruit in autumn. |
| May | Pearl Bush | Exochorda grandiflora | White | 5–6 ft. | Very pretty pearly white flowers. |
| Early April | Golden Bell | Forsythia | Yellow | 6–8 ft. | Long branches of golden, bell-shaped flowers. |
| May | Silver Bell | Halesia tetraptera | White | Tall | Very desirable. |
| September | Witch Hazel | Hamamelis Virginea | Yellow | 10 ft. | Flowers small. |
| Early summer | Hills of Snow | Hydrangea arborescens grandiflora | White | 3–5 ft. | Will thrive anywhere, even in shade. |
| Late summer | | Hydrangea paniculata grandiflora | White | 5–6 ft. | Cone-shaped flowers, changing to pink, then to bronze. |

# TABLE OF INFORMATION — JAMES KREWSON & SONS

| Time of Flowering | Common Name | Botanical Name | Color of Flower | Height | Remarks |
|---|---|---|---|---|---|
| July | | Hypericum | Yellow | Dwarf | Beautiful flowers in profusion at a season when flowers are scarce. |
| March | Jasmine | Jasminum nudiflorum | Yellow | 3-5 ft. | Flowers first mild days of spring. |
| May | Laurel | Kalmia latifolia | Rose-pink | | Thrives best in shade. |
| Late summer | Globe Flower | Kerria Japonica | Yellow | 3-5 ft. | Beautiful green bark. |
| June | Golden Chain | Laburnum | Yellow | Tall | |
| June | Regel's Privet | Ligustrum Regelianum | White | 2-3 ft. | Good foliage; bluish black berries in autumn. |
| | Golden Privet | Ligustrum variegatum | None | | Excellent, rich, golden foliage. |
| May | Bush Honeysuckle | Lonicera | Assorted | 4-6 ft. | Good erect grower; red berries in fall. |
| July, August | Bush Horse-Chestnut. | Pavia macrostachya | White | 6-8 ft. | |
| June | Mock Orange | Philadelphus coronarius | White | 6-8 ft. | Old-fashioned, sweet-scented Mock Orange. |
| June | Golden Mock Orange | Philadelphus coronarius aurea. | White | 3-5 ft. | Handsome golden foliage. |
| May | Japan Quince | Pyrus Japonica | Red and pink | 5-7 ft. | Sometimes called Fire Bush. |
| Spring | | Rhododendron | Assorted | Various | See Evergreen Shrubs. |
| May to frost | White Kerria | Rhodotypus Kerrioides | White | 5-7 ft. | A valuable shrub; thrives in hottest and driest situations. |
| July | Purple Fringe | Rhus Cotinus | Greenish purple | 10-12 ft. | Can be grown into small trees; very ornamental. |
| April | Flowering Currant | Ribes aureum | Yellow | 3-5 ft. | One of the sweetest-scented shrubs in cultivation; delicious spicy odor. |
| May | Rose Acacia | Robinia hispida | Rose-pink | 5-6 ft. | |
| Early summer | Japan Rose | Rosa rugosa | Red and white | 4-6 ft. | Hardy; excellent foliage; large scarlet seed-pods. |
| Early summer | Golden-leaved Elder | Sambucus nigra aurea | White | 5-7 ft. | Valued for its golden foliage. |
| Summer | | Spiræa, Anthony Waterer, callosa alba, Bumalda | Assorted | 2-3 ft. | See list of Shrubs. |
| April, May | | Spiræa arguta, Thunbergii. | White | 4-5 ft. | Have laciniated foliage. |
| May, June | | Spiræa opulifolia aurea, prunifolia, Reevesiana, Van Houttei. | Assorted | 5-7 ft. | See list of Shrubs. |
| July | | Spiræa sorbifolia | White | 5-7 ft. | Fern-like foliage, handsome and striking; showy spikes of flowers. |
| June | | Stephanandra flexuosa | Creamy white | 3-4 ft. | Grown for its foliage; assumes beautiful shades of bronze in autumn. |
| Midsummer | | Stuartia | White | Tall | Handsome, small tree; flowers resemble camellias. |
| May | Japan Silver Bell | Styrax Japonica | White | Tall | |
| May | Snowberry | Symphoricarpos racemosus | Pink | 3-4 ft. | Red flowers and white, wax-like berries. |
| | Lilac | Syringa | Assorted | | See list of Shrubs. |
| May | Tamarisk | Tamarix | Pink | Tall | Fast grower; should be severely pruned each year. |
| Late May | Arrowwood | Viburnum dentatum | Greenish white | 5-7 ft. | Fruit crimson, changing to black. |
| May | Wayfaring Tree | Viburnum Lantana | White | 6-8 ft. | Fruit red in autumn. |
| June | High-bush Cranberry | Viburnum Opulus | White | 8-10 ft. | Beautiful, large, red berries in autumn. |
| June | Snowball | Viburnum Opulus sterile | White | 8-10 ft. | Flowers double. Old-fashioned Snowball. |
| May | Japan Snowball | Viburnum plicatum | White | 8-10 ft. | Valuable; double and last longer than any other. |
| May | | Viburnum tomentosum | White | | Makes handsomest bush of all the Viburnums. Gets beautiful autumn coloring; scarlet berries. |
| June | | Weigela candida and nivea. | White | 5-7 ft. | |
| June to frost | | Weigela, Eva Rathke | Carmine-red | 4-5 ft. | Foliage turns rich reddish bronze in fall. |
| June | | Weigela floribunda | Red | 6-8 ft. | |
| June | | Weigela rosea | Pink | 6-8 ft. | Probably the best pink variety. |
| June | | Weigela Van Houttei | Carmine | 6-8 ft. | |
| June | | Weigela variegata | Pink | 4-5 ft. | Splendid variegated foliage entire summer. |

# INDEX

| | PAGE |
|---|---|
| Abies | 1, 2 |
| Acer | 11, 26 |
| Achillea | 29 |
| Adam's Needle | 32 |
| Æsculus | 12 |
| Agrostemma | 29 |
| Akebia | 27 |
| Almond, Flowering | 17 |
| Althæa | 20 |
| Alyssum | 29 |
| Amelanchier | 17 |
| Amorpha | 17 |
| Ampelopsis | 27 |
| Amygdalus | 17 |
| Andromeda | 8 |
| Anthemis | 29 |
| Apples | 33–35 |
| Apricots | 35 |
| Aquilegia | 29 |
| Aralia | 12 |
| Arborvitæ | 6, 7 |
| Aristolochia | 27 |
| Arrow-wood | 24 |
| Arundo | 28 |
| Ash | 14 |
| Ash, Mountain | 16 |
| Asimina | 12 |
| Aster, Cornflower | 32 |
| Asters | 29 |
| Astilbe | 29 |
| Aucuba | 8 |
| Azalea | 8, 17 |
| Baccharis | 17 |
| Balm of Gilead | 1, 15 |
| Bamboo | 28 |
| Barberry | 8, 17 |
| Beauty Fruit | 18 |
| Beech | 14 |
| Beech, Weeping | 26 |
| Bellflower, Chinese | 32 |
| Benzoin | 17 |
| Berberis | 8, 17 |
| Betula | 12 |
| Bignonia | 27 |
| Birch | 12 |
| Bittersweet | 27 |
| Blackberries | 38 |
| Bleeding Heart | 30 |
| Bluebird Flower | 32 |
| Boltonia | 29 |
| Boxwood | 9, 26 |
| Bridal Wreath | 22 |
| Buckeye | 12 |
| Buddleia | 17 |
| Button Bush | 18 |
| Buxus | 9, 26 |
| Calico Bush | 9 |
| Callicarpa | 18 |
| Calycanthus | 18 |
| Campanula | 29 |
| Candytuft | 30 |
| Canterbury Bells | 29 |
| Caragana | 18 |
| Carpinus | 13 |
| Caryopteris | 18 |
| Cassia | 18, 30 |
| Catalpa | 13, 26 |
| Ceanothus | 18 |
| Cedar | 2 |
| Cedar, Red | 3 |
| Cedrela | 13 |
| Cedrus | 2 |
| Celastrus | 27 |
| Cephalanthus | 18 |
| Cerasus | 13, 26 |
| Cercidiphyllum | 13 |
| Cercis | 13, 18 |
| Cherries | 35 |
| Cherry, Flowering | 13, 26 |
| Chionanthus | 19 |
| Chrysanthemum | 30 |
| Citrus | 19 |
| Cladrastis | 13 |
| Clematis | 27 |

| | PAGE |
|---|---|
| Clethra | 19 |
| Coffee Tree, Kentucky | 14 |
| Columbine | 29 |
| Colutea | 19 |
| Convallaria | 30 |
| Coreopsis | 30 |
| Cornus | 13, 19 |
| Corylus | 19 |
| Cowslip | 32 |
| Crab, Flowering | 15 |
| Cranberry, High-bush | 24 |
| Cratægus | 19 |
| Crab Apples | 35 |
| Cucumber Tree | 15 |
| Cupressus | 2 |
| Currant, Flowering | 22 |
| Currant, Indian | 23 |
| Currants | 38 |
| Cypress | 2 |
| Cypress, Deciduous | 16 |
| Cypress, Japan | 5, 6 |
| Cytisus | 13 |
| Daphne | 9 |
| Day Lily | 30 |
| Deciduous Shrubs | 17–24 |
| Deciduous Trees | 11–16 |
| Delphinium | 30 |
| Deutzia | 19 |
| Dianthus | 30 |
| Dielytra | 30 |
| Digitalis | 30 |
| Diospyros | 14 |
| Dogwood | 13, 19 |
| Dutchman's Pipe | 27 |
| Elder | 22 |
| Elder, Box | 11 |
| Elm | 16 |
| Elm, Weeping | 26 |
| Erianthus | 28 |
| Eulalia | 28 |
| Euonymus | 20 |
| Evergreen Shrubs | 8–10 |
| Evergreen Trees | 1–7 |
| Exochorda | 20 |
| Fagus | 14, 26 |
| Filbert | 38 |
| Fir | 1, 2 |
| Forsythia | 20 |
| Foxglove | 30 |
| Fraxinus | 14 |
| Fringe, White | 19 |
| Fruit Department | 33–38 |
| Funkia | 30 |
| Gaillardia | 30 |
| Garland Flower | 9 |
| Giant Tree of California | 7 |
| Ginkgo | 14 |
| Gleditschia | 14 |
| Golden Bell | 20 |
| Golden Chain | 21 |
| Golden Glow | 32 |
| Gooseberries | 38 |
| Grapes | 38 |
| Groundsel Bush | 17 |
| Gymnocladus | 14 |
| Halesia | 20 |
| Hamamelis | 20 |
| Hardy Grasses and Reeds | 28 |
| Hawkweed, Tawny | 30 |
| Hawthorn, English | 19 |
| Hazelnut | 38 |
| Hedera | 27 |
| Helianthus | 30 |
| Hemerocallis | 30 |
| Herbaceous Plants | 29–32 |
| Hercules' Club | 12 |
| Hibiscus | 20, 30 |
| Hieracium | 30 |
| Holly | 9 |
| Hollyhocks | 30 |
| Honeysuckle | 27 |
| Honeysuckle, Bush | 22 |
| Hornbeam | 13 |

| | PAGE |
|---|---|
| Horse-Chestnut | 12 |
| Horse-Chestnut, Bush | 22 |
| Hydrangea | 20 |
| Hypericum | 21 |
| Iberis | 30 |
| Ilex | 9 |
| Indigo, False | 17 |
| Iris | 31 |
| Ironwood | 13 |
| Ivy, English | 27 |
| Ivy, Japanese or Boston | 27 |
| Jasminum | 21 |
| Judas Tree | 13 |
| Judas Tree, Japan | 18 |
| Juneberry | 17 |
| Juniper | 2, 3 |
| Juniperus | 2, 3 |
| Kadsura, Japanese | 13 |
| Kalmia | 9 |
| Kerria | 21 |
| Kœlreuteria | 14 |
| Kudzu Vine | 27 |
| Laburnum | 21 |
| Larch | 14 |
| Larix | 14 |
| Laurel | 9 |
| Ligustrum | 21, 26 |
| Lilac | 23, 24 |
| Lily-of-the-Valley | 30 |
| Linden | 16 |
| Locust, Honey | 14 |
| Lonicera | 22, 27 |
| Lycium | 27 |
| Magnolia | 15 |
| Mahonia | 9 |
| Maidenhair Tree | 14 |
| Mallow | 30 |
| Maple | 11, 26 |
| Matrimony Vine | 27 |
| Mock Orange | 22 |
| Morus | 15, 26 |
| Mulberry | 15 |
| Mulberry, Weeping | 26 |
| Nuts | 38 |
| Oak | 16 |
| Orange, Hardy Japan | 19 |
| Oxydendrum | 15 |
| Pavia | 22 |
| Pawpaw | 12 |
| Pæonia | 31, 22 |
| Peaches | 35–37 |
| Peach, Flowering | 15 |
| Pearl Bush | 20 |
| Pears | 37 |
| Pea, Siberian | 18 |
| Pentstemon | 32 |
| Persica | 15 |
| Persimmon | 14 |
| Phalaris | 28 |
| Phlox | 32 |
| Philadelphus | 22 |
| Picea | 3, 4, 26 |
| Pine | 4, 5 |
| Pine, Umbrella | 6 |
| Pink, Mountain | 32 |
| Pinks | 30 |
| Pinus | 4, 5 |
| Plane | 15 |
| Plantain Lily | 30 |
| Platanus | 15 |
| Platycodon | 32 |
| Plum, Flowering | 15 |
| Plums | 38 |
| Podocarpus | 5 |
| Poplar | 15 |
| Populus | 15 |
| Primrose, English | 32 |
| Primula | 32 |
| Privet | 21, 26 |
| Prunus | 15 |
| Pueraria | 27 |
| Pyrethrum | 32 |
| Pyrus | 15, 22 |
| Quercus | 16 |

| | PAGE |
|---|---|
| Quinces | 38 |
| Raspberries | 38 |
| Red Bud | 13 |
| Red-hot Poker | 32 |
| Retinospora | 5, 6 |
| Rhododendrons | 10 |
| Rhus | 22 |
| Ribbon Grass | 28 |
| Ribes | 22 |
| Robinia | 22 |
| Rosa | 22 |
| Rose of Sharon | 20 |
| Roses | 25, 26 |
| Roses, Climbing | 27 |
| Rudbeckia | 32 |
| Salix | 16 |
| Sambucus | 22 |
| Sciadopitys | 6 |
| Sedum | 32 |
| Senna, Bladder | 19 |
| Senna, Wild | 18 |
| Shellbark | 38 |
| Silver Bell | 20 |
| Small Fruits | 38 |
| Smoke Bush | 22 |
| Snowball | 24 |
| Snowberry | 23 |
| Sophora | 16 |
| Sorbus | 16 |
| Sorrel Tree | 15 |
| Spice Bush | 17 |
| Spiderwort | 32 |
| Spiræa | 22, 23 |
| Spirea, Blue | 18 |
| Spirea, Herbaceous | 29 |
| Spruce | 3, 4 |
| Spruce, Hemlock | 7 |
| Spruce, Weeping | 26 |
| Stephanandra | 23 |
| Stokesia | 32 |
| Stonecrop, Giant | 32 |
| Stuartia | 23 |
| Styrax | 23 |
| Sunflower | 30 |
| Sweet Pepper Bush | 19 |
| Sweet Shrub | 18 |
| Sweet William | 30 |
| Symphoricarpos | 23 |
| Syringa | 23, 24 |
| Tamarisk | 24 |
| Tamarix | 24 |
| Taxodium | 16 |
| Taxus | 6 |
| Tea, New Jersey | 18 |
| Thorn, Cockspur | 19 |
| Thuya | 6, 7 |
| Tilia | 16 |
| Tradescantia | 32 |
| Tritoma | 32 |
| Trumpet Vine | 27 |
| Tsuga | 7 |
| Ulmus | 16, 26 |
| Umbrella Tree | 26 |
| Varnish Tree | 14 |
| Veronica | 32 |
| Viburnum | 24 |
| Vinca | 28 |
| Vines | 27, 28 |
| Virgilia | 13 |
| Walnut, Black | 38 |
| Walnut, English | 38 |
| Wayfaring Tree | 24 |
| Weeping and Formal Trees and Shrubs | 26 |
| Wellingtonia | 7 |
| Weigela | 24 |
| Willow | 16 |
| Wistaria | 28 |
| Witch Hazel | 20 |
| Yellow-wood | 13 |
| Yew | 6 |
| Yew, Japan | 5 |
| Yucca | 32 |

J. HORACE MCFARLAND COMPANY, HORTICULTURAL PRINTERS, HARRISBURG, PA.